MINIATURE CAKES, PASTRIES & DESSERTS

MINIATURE CAKES, PASTRIES & DESSERTS

PAM DOTTER

PEERAGE BOOKS

First published in Great Britain in 1986 by
Pelham Books Ltd

Created and produced by Phoebe Phillips Editions

This edition published in 1989 by
Peerage Books
Michelin House
81 Fulham Road
London SW3 6RB

ISBN 1 85052 150 6

Produced by Mandarin Offset
Printed and bound in Hong Kong

My thanks to the following for the help I have received in writing this book: my husband Frank who encouraged and tasted, Jacqui Hine who helped me develop and test the recipes then prepared the desserts so beautifully for photography, and Lynda Tyler and Joyce Weston for their help in typing the manuscript.

Contents

Introduction

The delicious, delectable desserts in this book are as good to look at as they are to eat, and can be combined to create a magical effect of light and colour on your table.

They reflect a new kind of cooking, for the very newest kind of dining. Today, no one wants to get up from a dinner table loaded down with excess cream and satiated with the over-rich taste of too much sweetness. People have learnt to eat well, and lightly. They appreciate that the subtle flavours and delicate charms of fine desserts are best enjoyed in small quantities. In the best of the new restaurants, too, clever *maîtres d'hôtel* suggest a mouthful of this and a tiny swirl of that, instead of heaping customers' plates with gargantuan slices of layer cake.

At home we do our guests an injury by expecting them to over-eat, especially of the deliciously sweet desserts most people love. But a single tiny tart can be the perfect ending to a meal, as can a bite of apple crumble, a coffeespoonful of lemon soufflé, a single fresh berry in a coating of richest chocolate.

A guest need not feel awkward refusing dessert, nor a hostess mortified because no one touches her dish of fruit fritters. Turn those fritters from thick slices of pineapple coated in batter, into individual mouthfuls – even a layer cake into tiny jewelled squares – and both guest and hostess will be happy.

With desserts created in miniature there is no need to stint on using the finest ingredients available, and the recipes that follow use light cream whips, exotic liqueurs, the tiniest of new fruits, smooth butters and chocolates, crisp pastries, melting chestnut purées and glistening crystallized fruits. Why not, when so little is required for each portion?

But there are also new ways of serving simple traditional favourites: Christmas puddings so small that their holly leaf decoration almost covers them; tiny golden sponge puddings; minute squares of glowing wine jellies; slivers of cheesecake.

Although these tend to be for more formal, festive occasions, other recipes in *Miniature Desserts* are just right for an informal dinner party with friends – what could be better than a choice of seasonal fruits, each berry or slice dipped in white and dark chocolate? The recipes are also useful for family meals: instead of baking huge rounds of cake, adapt a basic sponge recipe to make a variety of tiny morsels or create a selection of tartlets and flans from a single pastry recipe.

This introduction is followed by a chapter on making and serving miniature desserts, with ideas for suitable containers and other equipment and suggestions on how to combine and serve different kinds of dishes.

The chapters that follow are divided according to type of dessert – moulded, iced, cakes or biscuits, for instance – and, often, the main ingredient used – egg white in Meringues and Macaroons, for example, cream in Cream Desserts. Most chapters are further subdivided into various categories;

Moulded Desserts, for example, consists of cheesecakes, wine jellies and soufflés and mousses. And each category starts with a basic recipe highlighted in a tinted box. In turn, each of these recipes can be adapted to allow you to produce a range of variations on the basic theme.

Quantities for these basic recipes vary, according to what is practical. It is easier, for example, to handle a small amount of batter than the same amount of gelatine mixture which will set before you have time to divide it into individual portions. Many of the variations call for half, or even quarter, quantities of the basic recipe. In other cases, especially when an ingredient is replaced during making, each variation requires the 'full' amount of the basic recipe. Remember, though, that one of the greatest advantages of these miniature desserts is that the basic recipes can be multiplied, as well as divided, to give three or four parts that can be flavoured and shaped to produce from four to eight portions of three or four different desserts. If you freeze any left over after a dinner party, you will soon have a selection of miniature desserts to offer guests.

The number and size of portions that each recipe will yield is given in **bold type** above the list of ingredients. Remember though that these are miniature desserts, so a portion is by no means a serving – unless all your guests are on highly restricted diets.

Three or four portions should be enough for most people, but obviously, if your guests are hearty eaters, they will be tempted to try even more delicious recipes. If anyone is trying very hard to keep their calorie intake to a minimum, one perfect dessert will allow them a touch of luxury at the end of their meal, and still leave them feeling virtuous.

Ingredients for a number of desserts include items like icing, butter creams, custard, etc. Recipes for all these are highlighted with an asterisk, and given in detail in Creating Miniature Desserts, from page 147. If a 'made up' ingredient is a recipe in one of the main chapters, we give the page number.

Appearance is all-important when serving these tiny desserts, and ingredients include finishing touches like marzipan or chocolate leaves, frosted petals and other delights. These are also highlighted with an asterisk, and, like icings, etc are also given in full in Creating Miniature Desserts. In both cases, check with the index for exact page numbers if necessary.

Just two, final practical points:

I have given both imperial and metric measurements throughout. They are not interchangeable, so remember to use either one or the other.

Remember that cooking times may change slightly. The weather affects how quickly a jelly or a soufflé sets, the range of heat in your oven may vary when you are dealing with very small quantities of pastry, and microwave ovens must be used according to their instructions.

Making Miniature Desserts

Think small – in every way – if you want to succeed at creating, and making, miniature desserts. Start with unusual uses for standard kitchen equipment, and continue through practical matters like adapting freezing and storage methods for tiny quantities, to the most enjoyable aspect of this latest way of entertaining: combining different desserts to suit every occasion and every possible taste.

Equipment

All kinds of gadgets and kitchen equipment are available to make your task carefree and straightforward, and many utensils can be adapted to help you get professional results.

Preparation

Assemble your ingredients on plates before you begin cooking, so that you can see exactly what you have. If you do this, small quantities of spices and flavourings will not get lost.

Measuring spoons, from ¼ teaspoon (2.5ml spoon) capacity to a tablespoon (15ml) are a necessity, as are small wooden spoons. Use small plastic spoons to crush soft fruits lightly without absorbing the juice or the colourings.

Tea cups, or even egg cups, can be used for mixing small quantities.

A few small sieves, like the ones used for straining coffee, are useful for puréeing ingredients and sprinkling icing sugar. It is often – but not always – quicker and easier to sieve than liquidise in your normal electric machinery. Of course, if the quantity is large enough, and certainly if you are preparing for a large party, processors and liquidisers will be ideal.

When buying baking equipment, look at gadgets made for confectioners, and for making petits fours, available from specialist kitchenware shops.

Tiny moulds, in decorative shapes, are perfect for tartlets and puddings; aspic cutters are smaller than normal biscuit ones; or investigate the pleasant and unusual shapes available in stores' baking departments.

Learn to look searchingly at the most unlikely sources. Bottle caps make round shapes in a wide variety of sizes; large embroidery needles can be used to prick designs in miniature pie crusts; china sake cups hold tiny puddings for steaming – set them into small bamboo steamers, normally used for *dim sum*, Chinese dumplings.

Although most baking tins and moulds are too large for individual desserts, use the smallest flan size, usually about 4in (10cm), to make a single tart that can be divided into four or even six portions.

Mould cheesecakes in miniature bread tins, before slicing them. Half-filled, the tins are good containers for bar cakes, which can be sliced into thin portions.

Small yoghurt containers are ideal for moulding individual soufflés and gâteaux. Use baby food tins, open at one end, for steaming puddings or for setting jellies or other moulded desserts.

Choose small star piping tubes – the sort made for icing are ideal – for soft biscuit mixtures and eclairs.

Use small foil plates for pie crusts, and put them on a baking sheet so that they have some support in the oven.

If you cannot find any small cups for steaming, use egg cups instead. If you are handy with a pair of scissors, it is simple to cut through the side of a foil or waxed paper cup, overlap the sides so that the inside is much smaller, and then tape the outside together with masking tape. Crumple a little foil in a large cup to support this smaller version.

Use double thickness of heavy foil to mould containers of all shapes; form them on cosmetic jars and pill boxes – just look through the medicine chest and see what you can find.

Left Some of the ingredients used to make miniature desserts.

Serving

A selection of dolls' house furniture – tiny tables and sideboards, for example – makes delightful platters on which to serve one or two desserts.

Demitasse cups, in the very smallest size, are ideal containers for long biscuits. The saucers are usually both decorative and tiny; with a doily in the middle to disguise the indentation, they are perfect small plates. Coasters can also double as plates.

Little silver salt cellars can be called into use for glamorous dinner parties; use china versions for more informal family meals.

Use doilies to cover the centre holes in the glass and crystal bobèches that were set into candlesticks to keep the wax from dripping on to the table, and put a slice of cake on top of each.

Use melon ball scoops for ice creams and jellies. The small end of a double-sided scoop is ideal for fresh fruits.

Paper cases made for chocolates and petits fours will hold tartlets or slices of cake, and can also be used as moulds for chocolate cases.

Make foaming mousse desserts in the smallest available liqueur glasses instead of wine goblets, and use tiny coffee spoons for eating.

Serve tiny scoops of ice cream or sorbet in sherry glasses.

Planning Ahead

It makes good sense to have a selection of tiny desserts, or basic preparations like crusts and edible containers, ready to use.

Storage

Many of the basic recipes in the following chapters can be used to make different flavoured desserts, and freezing any that remain after a dinner party is a simple way to keep some for future use. Or put aside a few hours now and then to stock up your freezer; prepare the recipes to a stage where you will only need to add a few fresh ingredients and decorations to have desserts for any occasion.

Remember that tiny quantities freeze – and thaw – very quickly. If any of the larger gâteaux or desserts are to be divided, slice them while they are still half-frozen. Dessert 'basics' like cakes, crusts, crêpes and waffles can be made ahead in quantity, and frozen before they are filled or decorated. Choux pastry can be filled with whipped cream before freezing, although it will lose a little of its crispness.

Put sheets of plastic film between individual items so that they can be easily separated when you take them out of the freezer.

To freeze small, decorated cakes, simply stand them on a metal tray and let them get really hard before wrapping and labelling them.

Jellies and gelatine mixtures do not usually freeze very well – clear jellies collapse on thawing – but foamy mousses and soufflés can be frozen quite successfully if they are left in their original containers.

Biscuits, meringues and macaroons can be stored for up to six weeks in a closed box, provided it is really airtight. Use your freezer for longer storage.

Fruit cakes store very well for comparatively long periods, but remember to keep them moist – small sizes dry out quickly. A teaspoon (2.5ml spoon) of brandy added every week or so will do the trick.

Make fillings and creams ahead of time and store them separately in the freezer.

Decorative marzipan flowers, cut peel and toasted nuts can be made in large quantities and stored in airtight boxes.

Creative Combinations

Different desserts can be combined in all kinds of ways to match a variety of tastes and occasions. These are only a few suggestions.

French style A slither of Tarte Française, a taste of Meringue Belle Hélène, followed by Normandy Flan and Crème à la Coeur.

Crisp and crunchy Bite into Chocolate Cheesecake and tiny Ginger Nuggets, serve with Crunchnut Torten and Apple Crumble puddings.

Bittersweet delights Enjoy the contrast of Chocolate and Orange Roulade, Raspberries au Fromage and Coconut and Cheese Snaps.

Colourful berries Arrange Ripe Berry Tartlets with bright Spiced Blackberry and Apple Kissel, Blueberry Tarts, Red Berry Yoghurt Ice Cream and elegant Redcurrant Lilies.

Exotic fruits A scoop of Passion Fruit Water Ice, a dip into Banana and Rum Moscovite, a succulent spoonful of chilled Mango Soufflé, a portion of Glacé Fruit Bombe and a last lingering taste of Peach Melba.

Desserts for all seasons Conjure up New Year's Day with Athol Brose and festive Pecan Pie; round off the winter with Cherry Ripe Tartlets and Valentine Pavlovas; make delectable spring desserts of Peaches and Praline Cream mini-crêpes, Citrus Fruit Salad and Smooth Cheesecake Pie; celebrate summer with Rose Cream Meringues, and enter into the autumn spirit with St Clement's Creams and Golden Fruit Kissel.

Autumn harmony Blend the colours of Chocolate Chestnut Meringues with Chilled Ginger Soufflé, Walnut Coffee Tartlets with Flambéed Apricots, and contrast golden Syrup Puddings with Coffee Liqueur Granita.

Mid-summer surprise A taste of Chilled Zabaglione followed by Tropical Fruit Salad, Traditional Summer Pudding, cool Pina Colada Ice Cream, Rich Secret Desserts and refreshing Lemon Water Ice.

Eastern promise Taste the East with tangy Ginger and Yoghurt Moscovite, Maraschino Pyramid and Eastern Pearls; serve with Mango Slices, Harlequin Mallows, Tropical Surprises and Cinnamon-flavoured Danish Pastries.

Spring fever Get in the mood with Cherry Blossom Cheesecakes, Champagne Hearts, Rainbow Profiteroles, Apricot Pavlovas, Spiced Flowers and Green Fruit Salad.

Apples and pears Brandied Apple Fritters, Flambéed Pears, Apple and Raisin Danish Pastry, Pears with Gin and Lime Juice and Spiced Apple Crescents.

High spirits Kick off with Liqueur Barrels, Chestnut and Rum Ice Cream, Honey and Rum Babas and end up with Tipsy Peaches. Serve with Brandy Snaps.

Moulded Desserts

These beautifully shaped desserts range from clear, sparkling wine jellies set with fruits to fluffy creams, and shaped morsels and balls piled high in glasses. There are also tiny soufflées set in chocolate cups, delicate fruit mousses and creamy chilled cheesecakes.

Chilled Cheesecakes

Chilled, gelatine-based cheesecakes can be moulded and flavoured with fruit, chocolate and even chestnuts. They can be made creamy with full-fat soft cheese or less rich with curd cheese or quark. Use the basic chilled cheesecake recipe to make all the delicious desserts that follow.

Chilled Cheesecake

Two 4 × 4in (10 × 10cm) cheesecakes: 16 portions

For the bases
Two square 4in (10cm) Golden Crumb Crust bases (page 41)

Filling
½ ounce (15g) gelatine
4 ounces (100g) full-fat cream cheese
1 egg yolk
Grated rind of half a lemon
2 tablespoons (2 × 15ml spoons) caster sugar
¼ pint (125ml) soured or double cream

Place Golden Crumb Crust bases on a double thickness of foil large enough to extend 1in (2.5cm) up each side to form a box. Fold corners to neaten and secure.

Place gelatine in 3 tablespoons (3 × 15ml spoons) cold water in a small basin. Place basin over a pan of hot water or in a microwave oven for ½ minute to melt gelatine.

Place cream cheese, egg yolk, lemon rind and sugar in a medium bowl and beat until smooth. Gradually beat in the cream and the melted gelatine. Divide the mixture in half and flavour as in recipes that follow.

Pour the mixture on to prepared bases, level tops and chill until set. Carefully remove foil, gently running a hot knife between cheesecake and foil if necessary. Place cheesecakes on serving plates and decorate as desired.

Orange and Chocolate Cheesecake

One 4 × 4in (10 × 10cm) cheesecake; 8 portions

2 teaspoons (2 × 5ml spoons) finely grated orange rind
1 tablespoon (1 × 15ml spoon) orange juice
Orange food colouring
1 tablespoon (1 × 15ml spoon) finely chopped dessert chocolate
½ Chilled Cheesecake mixture
One square 4in (10cm) Golden Crumb Crust base (page 41)

Decoration
4 squares chocolate, melted
3 tablespoons (3 × 15ml spoons) whipped cream
8 Glazed Kumquat Slices*

Fold orange rind, juice, one or two drops of orange food colouring and the chocolate into the cheesecake mixture. Pour on to the base, prepared as for Chilled Cheesecake, and level top. Chill to set. Remove foil.

To decorate, place melted chocolate into a greaseproof-paper icing bag and drizzle chocolate over top of cheesecake. Pipe eight small rosettes of cream on the cheesecake and position a Glazed Kumquat Slice on top of each.

Previous pages, clockwise from left *Harlequin Mallow (page 25); 3in (7.5cm) Redcurrant Lily (page 24) surrounded by Chocolate Chestnut Meringues (opposite); Blackcurrant and Lychee Ring (page 20).*

Chocolate and Almond Cheesecake Gâteau

One 3 × 4in (8 × 10cm) gâteau; 6 portions

2 ounces (50g) dessert chocolate
½ Chilled Cheesecake mixture, omitting gelatine
18 ratafia biscuits
3 tablespoons (3 × 15ml spoons) rum or sherry

Decoration
2 tablespoons (2 × 15ml spoons) whipped cream
6 black cherries or grapes

Melt chocolate in a small basin over hot water. Stir into cheesecake mixture. Dip the biscuits in the rum or sherry for 30 seconds on each side.

Place a 4in (10cm) wide by 6in (15cm) long strip of greaseproof paper into a 3 × 4in (8 × 10cm) container to extend up the sides at either end for easy removal. Place six biscuits in the base and spread with half the mixture. Repeat with biscuits and mixture ending with a layer of biscuits. Cover and leave in the refrigerator overnight.

Lift out of mould, remove paper and place on a serving plate. Pipe a rosette of cream on each biscuit and place a cherry or grape on top. To serve, cut into six slices.

Chocolate Chestnut Meringues

Eight 2½in (6cm) meringues

3 tablespoons (3 × 15ml spoons) sweetened chestnut purée
1 Chilled Cheesecake mixture, using half the quantity of gelatine and omitting the egg yolk

Decoration
Mini Meringue Shells (page 122)
4 ounces (100g) chocolate, melted

Place a 1in (2.5cm) wide strip of greaseproof paper inside eight 2 fl oz (50ml) barrel-shaped moulds.

Beat the chestnut purée until smooth then fold into the cheesecake mixture. Divide the mixture between the moulds and leave to set.

Unmould the cheesecakes by inverting the mould and shaking each over a plate. Remove the paper. Place a Mini Meringue Shell each end of every cheesecake and pipe chocolate across the top of each one.

Cherry Blossom Cheesecakes

Six 1½in (4cm) cheesecakes

2 ounces (50g) maraschino cherries
½ Chilled Cheesecake mixture
1½ tablespoons (1½ × 15ml spoons) maraschino syrup from the jar or can

Decoration
6 – 8 ounces (150g – 200g) Green Marzipan*
Icing sugar
6 small ginger biscuits, about 1½in (4cm) in diameter
2 tablespoons (2 × 15ml spoons) kirsch
1 tablespoon (1 × 15ml spoon) chopped pistachio nuts

Finely chop cherries and fold into cheesecake mixture with syrup. Divide mixture between six 1½ fl oz (35ml) pots or egg cups. Leave to set.

Roll out marzipan and trim to 4 × 14in (10 × 35cm). Cut down its length into three 1¼in (3cm) strips, then cut twelve 1¼in (3cm) leaf shapes diagonally from each strip, six for each serving. Sprinkle six individual tartlet tins of 1 fl oz (25ml) capacity with icing sugar, then press the leaves, slightly overlapping, into each. Leave several hours or until the marzipan has set, then carefully remove from tins and leave to dry overnight.

Soak the biscuits in the kirsch for 30 seconds both sides then place one in each marzipan leaf case. Unmould cheesecakes and position one on top of each biscuit. Sprinkle pistachio nuts on top of each cheesecake to represent stamens.

A firmer cheesecake
Cheesecakes may also be made with curd cheese, which will give a slightly drier texture.

Wine Jellies

Wine jellies are remarkable for their adaptability and their delicate flavour. They can be used plain, flavoured or mixed with fruit, and moulded to almost any shape that strikes your fancy. Instead of white wine a rosé gives a delightful effect. If you use a dark or tawny dessert wine, on the other hand, fruit and purées will not show up so well, as the colour will be changed.

Wine Jelly

6 portions

½ pint (250ml) sweet white wine
1 ounce (25g) caster sugar
1 tablespoon (1 × 15ml spoon) lemon juice
½ ounce (15g) gelatine

Place wine, sugar and lemon juice in a scrupulously clean small saucepan and gently warm the mixture. Remove from heat, sprinkle in the gelatine, and leave 2 minutes to soften. Then stir over a low heat until the gelatine has dissolved. Do not boil. Strain into a measuring jug and leave jelly to cool.
   Use before setting point and flavour as required.

Cream Jelly

6 portions

Beat 3 ounces (75g) full-fat cream cheese with 2 tablespoons (2 × 15ml spoons) of the Wine Jelly until smooth. Beat in remaining jelly.

Blackcurrant Jelly

6 portions

Add 3 tablespoons (3 × 15ml spoons) blackcurrant syrup or Crème de Cassis liqueur to the Wine Jelly.

Jellied Fruit Salad

Six 2 fl oz (50ml) jellies

1 unset Wine Jelly
1 kiwi fruit
2 ounces (50g) wild strawberries (or small firm strawberries)

Decoration
Chantilly Cream (page 122)
6 wild (or small) strawberries with stalks

Set a little Wine Jelly in the bases of six 2 fl oz (50ml) moulds. Peel and slice kiwi fruit and cut slices into four or six pieces. Halve strawberries (or quarter if strawberries are larger). Layer a little fruit with a little jelly in the moulds, setting each layer in a cool place before adding the next. When the moulds are full leave to set firmly.
   Dip the moulds in hand-hot water and invert on to cold plates.
   Pipe a rosette of Chantilly Cream on top of each one and decorate with a strawberry. Use the day it is made.

A firm jelly
Never allow the gelatine to boil or you will spoil its setting quality.

Left *Maraschino Pyramid (page 20) served in a liqueur glass.*

Maraschino Pyramid

Six 2 fl oz (50ml) pyramids

2 ounces (50g) maraschino cherries
1 unset Cream Jelly, as recipe (page 19)
1 tablespoon (1 × 15ml spoon) caster sugar

Decoration
2 ounces (50g) maraschino cherries
2 tablespoons (2 × 15ml spoons) maraschino syrup

Finely chop 2 ounces (50g) cherries and stir into unset Cream Jelly with the sugar. Pour into a small, deep container and leave to set.

To make the sauce, liquidize the cherries with the syrup, then press the purée through a nylon sieve.

Form the set jelly into balls with a warmed melon baller, place on a metal tray and chill until firm. (Melt the remaining jelly over warm water and repeat.)

To serve, stack the balls in pyramids in six tiny bowl-shaped glasses and trickle the sauce over them.

Blackcurrant and Lychee Rings

Six 1½ in (4cm) rings

1 unset Blackcurrant Jelly, as recipe (page 19)
6 ounces (150g) fresh or 4 ounces (100g) canned
*   lychees*

Decoration
Frosted Mint Leaves*

Pour jelly into six 2 fl oz (50ml) ring moulds and chill until set. Peel lychees and remove the stones. Chop half the fruit and reserve for decoration. Liquidize remaining fruit.

To serve, dip moulds in hand-hot water, invert on to six small chilled plates. Fill the centres with chopped lychees and decorate with Frosted Mint Leaves. Pour a little lychee sauce around each and chill until ready to serve.

Eastern Pearls

Six 2 fl oz (50ml) portions

½ pint (250ml) skimmed milk
½ ounce (15g) gelatine
Flavouring (see below)

Decoration
6 fresh mango slices
6 kiwi fruit slices
1 ounce (25g) chopped pistachio nuts

Place the milk in a scrupulously clean small saucepan and warm gently. Remove from the heat, sprinkle in the gelatine, and leave 2 minutes to soften. Then stir over a low heat until the gelatine has dissolved. Do not boil. Strain into a measuring jug and leave jelly to cool. Place a flavouring and colouring in three small basins and add one-third of the milk jelly to each. Pour into three rectangular plastic containers about 4in × 5in (10 × 12.5cm) and chill until set.

Cut jelly into small squares in each container and invert each on to wetted greaseproof paper; tap the bottom of the containers to release the jelly.

Arrange mixed cubes in six bowl-shaped sherry glasses with the mango and kiwi fruit slices. Sprinkle with pistachio nuts.

Almond
1 tablespoon (1 × 15 ml spoon) Amaretto liqueur or a few drops almond extract and a drop of green food colouring.

Rose
A few drops of rosewater and a drop of pink food colouring.

Coffee
1 tablespoon (1 × 15ml spoon) Tia Maria liqueur or ½ teaspoon (2.5ml spoon) instant coffee dissolved in 1 teaspoon (1 × 5ml spoon) boiling water.

How to chop jelly
Place jelly on wetted greaseproof paper on a chopping board. Use a hot or wet knife to chop the jelly.

Soufflés and Mousses

Egg whites add air to soufflés, while mousses are lightened with whipped cream. Both can be flavoured and shaped in all kinds of ways. The recipes that follow include soufflés in chocolate cases, and variations on fruit-based mousses. Take care to fold the flavourings in gently using a metal spoon to avoid spoiling the delicate texture.

Chilled Soufflé

6 portions

2 teaspoons (2 × 5ml spoons) gelatine
1 teaspoon (1 × 5ml spoon) grated lemon
*   rind*
2 eggs, separated
3 level tablespoons (3 × 15ml spoons)
*   caster sugar*
3 fluid ounces (75ml) double cream

Place gelatine with 2 tablespoons (2 × 15ml spoons) cold water in a small basin and dissolve over a pan of hot water. Leave to cool.

Place lemon rind, egg yolks and sugar (together with flavour as below) in a basin over hot water and whisk until mixture is thick and creamy. Remove from heat and whisk until cool. Whisk in gelatine.

Whip egg whites and cream separately until they just hold their shape, then fold into the mixture. Pour into containers and leave to set.

Vanilla
Whisk in 1 teaspoon (1 × 5ml spoon) vanilla extract or use Vanilla Sugar*.

Chocolate
Melt 2 ounces (50g) plain chocolate in a small basin over hot water, and whisk in with the egg yolks.

Lemon
Whisk in the grated rind and juice of 1 lemon with the egg yolks. For lemon tang soufflé replace the cream with soured cream or natural yoghurt.

Orange
Whisk in the grated rind and juice of half an orange (small), and 1 tablespoon (1 × 15ml spoon) lemon juice. Tint pale orange with food colouring.

Lime
Whisk in the grated rind and juice of 1 lime and half a lemon. Tint pale green with food colouring.

Ginger
Chop 6 pieces of stem ginger and fold in with 1 tablespoon (1 × 15ml spoon) ginger syrup from the jar.

Apricot
Make apricot purée by liquidizing canned or cooked fresh apricots. Add ¼ pint (125ml) to soufflé mixture with the egg yolks.

Mango
As apricot, using peeled sieved mangoes.

Ingredients, sauces, edible containers, etc that are asterisked in the recipes on these pages are given in detail on pages 147 to 156. For exact page numbers, refer to the index at the end of the book.

Cup Soufflés

Six 2 fl oz (50ml) soufflés

6 Chocolate Cases*, using small paper cake cases
1 Chilled Soufflé mixture (page 21)

Prepare the 'cups' before making the soufflé.

Place a 1in (2.5cm) wide piece of double foil round the top edge of each Chocolate Case to make a 'collar' above the case. Make a little fold to secure. Fill with soufflé-mixture and chill until set. Carefully remove the collars by running a hot knife between the foil and soufflé.

Lemon Cup Soufflés

Six 2 fl oz (50ml) soufflés

1 Chilled Soufflé mixture with lemon flavour (page 21)
6 Chocolate Cases*

Decoration
2 tablespoons (2 × 15ml spoons) whipped cream
Pinch of Glazed Lemon Peel Strands*
1 slice lemon

Make Cup Soufflés as described in previous recipe.

Remove foil and decorate with lemon strands. Cut the lemon slice in half and arrange on the plate.

Lime or Orange Cup Soufflés

Replace lemon flavour Chilled Soufflé mixture with lime or orange flavour (page 21), and replace lemon slice and strands with lime or orange slices and strands.

Ginger Cup Soufflé

Six 2 fl oz (50ml) soufflés

6 Chocolate Cases*
1 Chilled Soufflé with ginger flavour (page 21)

Decoration
2 tablespoons (2 × 15ml spoons) whipped cream
6 slices stem ginger
24 piped Chocolate Shapes*

Make up Cup Soufflés as described, and remove foil collars.

Decorate with piped cream, ginger pieces and Chocolate Shapes.

Lime Charlottes

Six 2 fl oz (50ml) charlottes

1 Chilled Soufflé mixture with lime flavour (page 21)

Decoration
36 coffee-flavoured 'matchsticks'
2 fl oz (50ml) Chantilly Cream (page 122)
1 1/2 slices of fresh lime
Narrow green ribbon

Pour soufflé into six 2 fl oz (50 ml) dariole moulds or straight-sided round plastic moulds. Leave to set. Turn moulds out on to cold plates.

Cut matchsticks to height of moulds and press round the sides to cover. Tie a piece of ribbon round each charlotte. Pipe small rosettes of Chantilly Cream round the top edges of the soufflés and decorate with small pieces of lime.

Mango Slices

Two 1/4 pint (125ml) soufflés; 12 slices

1 Chilled Mango Soufflé mixture (page 21) using 2 teaspoons (2 × 5ml spoons) honey instead of sugar
Replace the whipped cream in the basic mixture with 1/4 pint (125ml) natural yoghurt
4 tablespoons (4 × 15ml spoons) mango purée

Decoration
1 teaspoon (1 × 5ml spoon) gelatine
A few pieces of very thinly sliced mango

To make the decoration, first place the gelatine in 2 tablespoons (2 × 15ml spoons) cold water in a small basin. Melt over a pan of hot water or in a microwave oven. Spoon a little into the bases of two 1/4-pint (125ml) oblong containers such as metal bread tins. Leave to set then arrange mango pieces on it. Cover with a thin layer of the jelly and leave to set.

Spoon soufflé mixture into prepared moulds. Leave to set. Turn moulds out on to a cold plate and chill before slicing.

Serve two slices for each portion on chilled plates. Decorate with mango pieces.

Right, from top *2 fl oz (50ml) Lemon, Lime and Orange Cup Soufflés (opposite).*

Fruit Mousse

6 portions

2 teaspoons (2 × 5ml spoons) gelatine
¼ pint (125ml) fruit purée
2 teaspoons (2 × 5ml spoons) lemon juice
¼ pint (125ml) double or whipping cream

Place gelatine with 3 tablespoons (3 × 15ml spoons) cold water in a small basin. Melt over a pan of hot water or in a microwave oven. Leave to cool; then stir into fruit purée with lemon juice.

Whip cream until it just holds its shape and fold it into the fruit purée. Pour into mould and leave to set.

Dip mould in hand-hot water and invert on to a chilled plate.

Redcurrant Lilies

Six 3 × 3in (7.5cm) lilies

8 ounces (200g) redcurrants
1 unset Fruit Mousse mixture

Decoration
6 ounces (150g) filo pastry
2 tablespoons (2 × 15ml spoons) sugar
Small bunches of Frosted Redcurrants (page 97)

Cook redcurrants in a ¼ pint (125ml) water in a covered saucepan over a low heat until soft. Drain, reserving juice, then sieve fruit. Stir purée into mousse mixture. Divide the mixture between six 2½ fl oz (60ml) moulds and leave to set.

Heat the oven to 375°F, 190°C, Gas Mark 5. Grease the outside of six over-turned ovenproof cups. Cut the filo pastry into 18 squares of 4 × 4in (10 × 10cm) and drape three squares loosely over each cup without letting the pastry stick to the sides. Bake 10 to 12 minutes until crisp and golden. Leave to cool then carefully remove from cups.

Dissolve sugar in ¼ pint (125ml) redcurrant juice over a medium heat then bring to the boil and continue boiling until juice is reduced by half. Cool.

Unmould redcurrant mousses and place one in each pastry case. Drizzle a little sauce over them and place a bunch of Frosted Redcurrants on each case.

Chocolate-Centred Chestnut Mousses

Six 2½ fl oz (60ml) mousses

1 unset Fruit Mousse mixture, made with 4 tablespoons (4 × 15ml spoons) sweetened chestnut purée and juice of ½ orange instead of fruit purée
2 ounces (50g) dessert chocolate
2 teaspoons (2 × 5ml spoons) dark rum

Decoration
2 tablespoons (2 × 15ml) sweetened chestnut purée
6 maraschino cherries

Using half the chestnut mousse mixture, divide between six 2½ fl oz (60ml) deep moulds or tiny after-dinner coffee cups.

Melt the chocolate in a small basin over a pan of hot water. Stir into remaining chestnut mousse, with the rum. Place the mixture into a nylon piping bag with a large plain tube and pipe it into the centres of the moulds. Leave to set.

With a small tube, pipe sweetened chestnut purée in ribbons on to serving plates making six circles slightly larger than the moulds. Dip the moulds into hand-hot water; invert one in the centre of each chestnut ring. Place a cherry on each.

To unmould mousses and soufflés
Loosen edge of mould with fingertips and dip mould into a bowl of hand-hot water. Take it out almost immediately and place a plate over the mould, then invert mould and plate and shake gently. When dessert has been released, carefully remove mould to avoid damaging the surface.

Gooseberry Mousses

Six 2½ fl oz (60ml) mousses

Green food colouring
1 unset Fruit Mousse mixture made with gooseberry
*   purée*

Decoration
6 Macaroon Fingers (page 129)
¼ pint (125ml) pouring cream

Stir a little food colouring into the mousse and set the mixture in six 2½ fl oz (60ml) ice-lolly moulds.

Unmould on to cold plates and place a Macaroon Finger into each one to represent a stick. Serve with cream.

Harlequin Mallows

Eight 2½ fl oz (60ml) mallows

8 white marshmallows
4 red glacé cherries
2 green glacé cherries
1 unset Fruit Mousse made with ¼ pint (125ml)
*   apple purée*

Decoration
5 pink marshmallows
3 tablespoons (3 × 15ml spoons) pale dry sherry
6 tablespoons (6 × 15ml spoons) double cream,
*   whipped*
Pink food colouring
Pink Chocolate Butterflies*

Snip the marshmallows into small pieces with wetted scissors. Chop the red and green cherries and fold into the mousse with the marshmallows. Divide mixture between eight 2½ fl oz (60ml) moulds or cups and leave to set in the refrigerator.

Place the pink marshmallows and sherry in a small basin and melt over hot water or in a microwave oven. Fold into the whipped cream and tint pink with food colouring.

To serve, dip moulds into warm water and turn mousses out on to chilled plates. Coat each with marshmallow cream pulled up in soft peaks. Decorate each with a Pink Chocolate Butterfly.

China moulds
To remove a mousse from a china mould, hold it in hand-hot water for the count of 20, to allow the warmth to penetrate.

Champagne Hearts

Six 2½ fl oz (60ml) hearts

½ pound (250g) pink champagne rhubarb
3 ounces (75g) sugar
1 Fruit Mousse recipe, but excluding fruit purée

Decoration
2 teaspoons (2 × 5ml spoons) gelatine
Pink or red food colouring
Frosted Rose Petals*
¼ pint (125ml) pouring cream

Cook rhubarb with 4 tablespoons (4 × 15ml spoons) water and the sugar. Drain into a measuring jug, pressing out the juice. Reserve. Liquidize or sieve the fruit.

Fold rhubarb purée into the mousse mixture then pour into six 2½ fl oz (60ml) heart-shaped moulds and leave to set.

Heat ¼ pint (125ml) rhubarb juice in a small pan until warm, then sprinkle the gelatine over it and leave for 2 minutes. Stir over a low heat until dissolved. Add a few drops of food colouring.

Spoon a little of this jelly over six serving plates and leave to set. Unmould the hearts on to the plates on top of the jelly and decorate with Frosted Rose Petals. Serve with cream.

Liqueur Barrels

Two ¼ pint (125ml) barrels; 6 portions

2 tablespoons (2 × 15ml spoons) icing sugar
1 unset Fruit Mousse mixture made without fruit
1 tablespoon (1 × 15ml spoon) Tia Maria liqueur
1 tablespoon (1 × 15ml spoon) Grand Marnier
Orange food colouring

Decoration
2 ounces (50g) Toasted Chopped Hazelnuts*
2 ounces (50g) Toasted Chopped Almonds*
3 tablespoons (3 × 15ml spoons) whipped cream

Stir icing sugar into mousse mixture and divide equally into two bowls. Stir Tia Maria into one bowl and Grand Marnier with a drop of orange food colouring into the other; pour each into a ¼-pint (125ml) cylindrical mould or tin. Cool to set.

Dip moulds into hand-hot water and unmould mousses on to wetted greaseproof paper.

Roll the Tia Maria mousse in chopped hazelnuts to coat and the Grand Marnier one in the almonds. Return to the refrigerator to chill well.

Cut into slices and decorate with the cream.

Cream Desserts

Flavour these velvety desserts with delicate fruits, rich chocolate or liqueurs and serve in elegant glasses, or form edible containers from biscuit, chocolate or marzipan. This chapter also contains a recipe for zabaglione – a creamy dessert made from egg yolks.

Fruit Fools

Smooth fruit purée blended into whipped cream makes a simple yet delicious dessert. Variations include adding fruit juices, liqueurs and even sponge cake.

Fruit Fool

About 1 pint (500ml); six portions

½ pint (250ml) double cream
2 tablespoons (2 × 15ml spoons) lemon juice
4 tablespoons (4 × 15ml spoons) icing sugar
½ pint (250ml) fruit purée

Place the cream, lemon juice and icing sugar in a chilled bowl. Whisk until it just holds its shape. Gradually whisk in the fruit purée and continue whisking until the mixture is thick.

Divide between six small glasses. Decorate and chill for one hour.

Serve with Brandy Snaps (page 65) or other crisp biscuits.

Syllabub

Six 3 fl oz (75ml) portions

1 egg white
2 fluid ounces (50ml) Grand Marnier
2 fluid ounces (50ml) fresh orange juice
½ quantity Fruit Fool recipe, but omitting fruit purée
6 Brandy Snaps (page 65)

Whisk egg white until it just holds its shape. Stir Grand Marnier and orange juice together in a jug. Gradually whisk juice into fool recipe and continue whisking until mixture just holds its shape. Fold in egg white. Divide between six small glasses.

Chill for 30 minutes. Serve with a Brandy Snap.

Tipsy Peaches

Six filled peach halves

3 firm, fresh peaches (or 6 halves from a can)
3 tablespoons (3 × 15ml spoons) orange juice
1 tablespoon (1 × 15ml spoon) kirsch
3 tablespoons (3 × 15ml spoons) honey
A few drops almond extract
1 fluid ounce (25ml) freshly filtered black coffee
1 fluid ounce (25ml) brandy
½ quantity Fruit Fool recipe, but omitting fruit purée

Decoration
2 slices kiwi fruit

Halve peaches and discard stones (or drain canned peaches). Place orange juice, kirsch, honey and almond extract in a shallow saucepan over a low heat and stir until the honey has dissolved. Increase heat, add peaches and simmer gently for a few minutes, turning them over once, until the syrup has evaporated. Leave peaches to cool, then drain them on kitchen paper and remove the skins.

Gradually whisk coffee and brandy into fool mixture and continue whisking until thick. Place mixture in a piping bag fitted with a large star tube.

Place peaches, cut side uppermost, on six small serving plates, cutting a little off the bottom of each peach to make it sit firmly. Pipe a large swirl of fool mixture in the centre of each peach. Chill for 30 minutes. Cut each kiwi slice in three and place one slice on each portion.

Previous pages, clockwise from left *Chocolate Pots (page 32); Tipsy Peach (right); Athol Brose (opposite); 2½in (6cm) Crème à la Coeur (page 33).*

Ingredients, sauces, edible containers, etc that are asterisked in the recipes on these pages are given in detail on pages 147 to 156. For exact page numbers, refer to the index at the end of the book.

Athol Brose

Six 3 fl oz (75ml) portions

1 ounce (25g) medium oatmeal
1 ounce (25g) blanched almonds, finely chopped
2 tablespoons (2 × 15ml spoons) lemon juice
2 tablespoons (2 × 15ml spoons) whisky
1 tablespoon (1 × 15ml spoon) clear honey
½ quantity Fruit Fool recipe, but omitting fruit
  purée
Rind of 1 small lemon

Decoration
6 strawberries, halved

Toast oatmeal and almonds under a medium-hot grill until evenly browned.

Stir lemon juice and whisky into the honey. Place fool mixture in a medium bowl and gradually add honey mixture; continue whisking until it is thick. Fold in the nuts, oatmeal and lemon rind.

Place mixture in a piping bag fitted with a large star potato tube and pipe into six swirls in small glasses. Decorate with halved strawberries.

Avocado and Orange Cups

Six 2 fl oz (50ml) cups

1 ripe avocado
Grated rind and juice of 1 small orange
½ quantity Fruit Fool recipe, but omitting fruit
  purée
Green food colouring (optional)
*6 Chocolate Cases**
4 tablespoons (4 × 15ml spoons) whipped Chantilly
  Cream (page 122)
2 kumquats, finely sliced
12 Ratafias (page 61)

Halve avocado, discard stone, scoop out flesh and liquidize with the orange juice and rind until smooth, or press through a sieve. Quickly whisk the purée into the basic fool mixture with a little food colouring, if desired. Whisk until thick.

Divide the mixture between the Chocolate Cases and chill for 30 minutes.

Decorate with small rosettes of Chantilly Cream and slices of kumquat. Serve with Ratafias.

St Clement's Creams

Six 4 fl oz (100ml) portions

2 ounces (50g) sponge cake
1 small orange
1 small lemon
½ quantity Fruit Fool recipe, but omitting fruit
  purée

Decoration
*Glazed Orange and Lemon Peel Strands**

Crumble cake and place crumbs in six small pots or glasses. Grate rind of fruit. Squeeze juice from orange and lemon and mix them together in a jug. Gradually whisk juices into the fool mixture in a small bowl and continue whisking until the mixture holds its shape. Stir in the grated rinds.

Divide between pots and tap on a hard surface to settle contents. Chill for several hours or overnight to let the juices soak into the sponge. Decorate with Orange and Lemon Peel Strands.

Rhubarb and Ginger Layers

Six 3 fl oz (75ml) portions

1 lb (500g) prepared rhubarb
2 tablespoons (2 × 15ml spoons) syrup from jar of
  stem ginger
2 tablespoons (2 × 15ml spoons) caster sugar
2 pieces stem ginger
6 small French Meringues (page 120)
½ quantity Fruit Fool recipe, but omitting fruit
  purée
*2 ounces (50g) Toasted Chopped Hazelnuts**
6 Brandy Snaps (page 65)

Place rhubarb, ginger syrup and sugar in a medium pan, cover and cook over a low heat until the rhubarb is soft. Drain and press through a sieve to make a purée. Finely chop the ginger and crumble the meringues. Place a rounded teaspoon (5ml spoon) rhubarb purée in the base of each glass.

Place half the fool mixture into a piping bag fitted with a large star tube and whisk the remaining rhubarb into the remaining fool mixture.

Reserve a little ginger for decoration and fold remainder into rhubarb mixture. Divide half this mixture between the glasses and sprinkle meringues over it with half the nuts. Spoon the remaining rhubarb mixture, then the nuts into the glasses. Pipe a large swirl of Fruit Fool mixture on top of each and sprinkle the remaining ginger over.

Chill 1 hour. Serve with a Brandy Snap.

Custard Creams

This rich, creamy base can be flavoured in many ways and set in tiny glasses or edible containers. Nuts and citrus strands complement its smooth texture.

Custard Cream

About 1½ pints (750ml); 12 portions

1 orange
½ pint (250ml) milk
2 egg yolks
2 ounces (50g) caster sugar
2 tablespoons (2 × 15ml spoons) cornflour
1 egg white, whisked
½ pint (250ml) double cream, whipped

Remove rind from orange with a potato peeler and place in a small pan with the milk. Heat slowly to boiling point. Leave to cool.

Place yolks, sugar and cornflour in a small bowl and beat together until pale and creamy. Gradually stir in the strained milk. Return mixture to the pan and whisk over a medium heat until mixture thickens and boils. Simmer for 1 minute. Remove from heat and continue whisking until the custard is cool. Beat in flavouring, then fold in the egg white and cream. Chill before serving.

Prune Velvets

Six 3 fl oz (75ml) portions

4 ounces (100g) pitted prunes
½ pint (250ml) freshly made tea
1 lemon
½ quantity Custard Cream recipe
Glazed Lemon Peel Strands*
Toasted Chopped Hazelnuts*
4 Orange and Almond Cigars (page 66)

Place prunes in the tea. Remove lemon rind with a potato peeler, add to prunes and leave to soak several hours or overnight until prunes are swollen and soft. Drain and liquidize the prunes, using a little juice if necessary, to make 4 fluid ounces (100ml) purée.

Whisk custard mixture and gradually whisk in prune purée. Divide between four small glasses. Chill. Decorate with lemon strips and nuts. Serve with Orange and Almond Cigars.

Mango Creams

Six 2½ fl oz (60ml) portions

4 fluid ounces (100ml) mango purée
½ quantity Custard Cream recipe
A few drops orange food colouring (optional)
2 ounces (50g) marzipan
2 tablespoons (2 × 15ml spoons) chopped pecan nuts
6 pecan nut halves
6 Brandy Snaps (page 65)

Whisk mango purée into the Custard Cream, adding a few drops of food colouring if desired.

Grate the marzipan and place in six small serving glasses. Place a little Custard Cream on top and then a layer of chopped nuts. Top with remaining custard. Chill before serving. Decorate each with a pecan nut half and serve with a Brandy Snap.

Pineapple and Walnut Cones

Six 3in (7.5cm) cones

2 ounces (50g) fresh or canned pineapple
1 ounce (25g) shelled walnuts
1 ounce (25g) crystallized ginger
½ quantity Custard Cream recipe
6 Coupelle Cornets (page 65)
2 small pieces crystallized ginger, sliced
2 glacé cherries, chopped

Drain the pineapple on kitchen paper and finely chop. Finely chop walnuts and ginger. Fold pineapple, walnuts and ginger into Custard Cream mixture. Divide the mixture between six Coupelle Cornets and serve at once decorated with sliced ginger and chopped cherries.

Right, from top *Paska (page 33); 3in (7.5cm) Summer Fruit Basket (page 33); Tropical Surprise (page 33).*

Chilled Zabaglione

Four 2½ fl oz (60ml) portions

2 egg yolks
2 ounces (50g) sugar
3 fluid ounces (75ml) sweet white wine, Marsala or sherry

To serve
4 ounces (100g) fraises des bois or raspberries
4 Langues des Chats (page 64)

Fill a saucepan about one-third full of water and place a round-bottomed bowl over the pan to ensure that the water does not touch the bottom of the bowl. Remove bowl and bring pan of water to the boil.

Place yolks and sugar in the bowl and, using a small balloon whisk, beat mixture until pale and thick. Set bowl over the prepared pan and pour wine into the eggs and sugar. Reduce heat and do not allow water to rise above a slow simmer.

Using the balloon whisk, beat mixture continually for about 15 minutes until it is thick and has doubled in volume.

Remove bowl from pan and place in a bowl of cold or iced water. Continue whisking occasionally until custard has cooled.

Divide fraises des bois between four small glasses, reserving a few for decoration. Pour zabaglione over fruit and chill for 30 minutes before serving. (To serve warm, whisk over boiling water for about 3 minutes and spoon into tall glasses, omitting fruit.)

Place a Langue de Chat by each portion.

Chocolate Pots

Six 3½ fl oz (80ml) portions

½ quantity Custard Cream recipe (page 30)
3 ounces (75g) dark dessert chocolate
2 tablespoons (2 × 15ml spoons) dark rum
1 tablespoon (1 × 15ml spoon) freshly filtered strong coffee
¼ pint (125ml) double cream, whipped
Chocolate coffee bean sweets or Chocolate Motifs*

To serve
12 Langues des Chats (page 64)

Make Custard Cream recipe up to the stage where custard is cooked.

Remove the mixture from the heat. Grate the chocolate and stir into the custard until melted. Beat in rum and coffee and continue beating until the mixture is cool.

Fold in egg white and cream from basic Custard Cream recipe.

Place half the whipped cream in a piping bag fitted with a star tube and put in a cool place to use for decoration.

Fold remaining cream into the chocolate mixture and divide between the serving pots. Tap pots gently on a hard surface in order to settle the contents. Chill.

Pipe a swirl of cream on each pot and add a chocolate decoration.

Serve with the Langues des Chats.

Soft Cheese Creams

This light yet tangy mixture tastes like cheesecake. Replace the full-fat cheese with low-fat soft cheese to reduce calories.

Soft Cheese Creams

Twelve 1½ fl oz (40ml) portions

6 ounces (150g) full fat soft cream cheese
1 ounce (25g) icing sugar
1 tablespoon (1 × 15ml spoon) lemon juice
Grated rind of ½ lemon
¼ pint (125ml) whipping cream, whipped
1 egg white, whipped

Beat cheese until soft. Add icing sugar, lemon juice and rind, and beat until smooth.

Beat in flavouring as in the recipes on the opposite page.

Whisk in cream and egg white.

Pipe or swirl the mixture into small containers. Chill in the refrigerator for at least 30 minutes before serving.

Tropical Surprises

Six 2½ fl oz (60ml) portions

2 ounces (50g) raisins
2 tablespoons (2 × 15ml spoons) fresh orange juice
2 tablespoons (2 × 15ml spoons) dark rum
1 firm, ripe banana
½ quantity Soft Cheese Cream recipe
6 Marzipan Flowers*

Decoration
1 teaspoon (1 × 5ml spoon) chopped pistachio nuts

Place raisins, orange juice and rum in a small pan and heat gently but do not boil (or heat in a microwave oven). Leave raisins to cool in the liquid.

Mash banana and whisk into the Soft Cheese Cream mixture. Leave to chill for 30 minutes.

Drain raisins and divide them between 6 Marzipan Flowers. Place the banana mixture in a piping bag, fitted with a large plain tube, and pipe mixture into the centre of each flower. Decorate with nuts. Serve at once.

Summer Fruit Baskets

Six 3in (7.5cm) baskets

4 ounces (100g) redcurrants
2 tablespoons (2 × 15ml spoons) caster sugar
2 tablespoons (2 × 15ml spoons) water
2 tablespoons (2 × 15ml spoons) Drambuie liqueur
½ quantity Soft Cheese Cream recipe
6 Chocolate Cases*

To serve
6 Chocolate Leaves*

Remove stalks from redcurrants. Dissolve sugar gently in the water in a small pan or microwave oven. Bring to boil and cook 1 minute. Remove from heat and stir in Drambuie.

Pour syrup over redcurrants and leave for 1 hour, occasionally stirring. Drain fruit well on kitchen paper.

Whisk 1 tablespoon (15ml spoon) of the syrup into the Soft Cheese Cream, place in a piping bag fitted with a star tube and pipe the mixture into the Chocolate Cases, leaving a hole in the centre. Chill for 30 minutes before serving.

Fill centres with redcurrants and drizzle a little syrup over. Decorate with Chocolate Leaves. Serve any remaining redcurrants around the base of the baskets.

Paska

Six 3in (7.5cm) portions

1 ounce (25g) small raisins
1 tablespoon (1 × 15ml spoon) lemon juice
2 teaspoons (2 × 5ml spoons) Amaretto liqueur
1 ounce (25g) blanched almonds
1 ounce (25g) glacé cherries (red and green)
1 ounce (25g) candied fruit peel
1 ounce (25g) crystallized ginger
1 ounce (25g) crystallized pineapple
½ quantity Soft Cheese Cream recipe, omitting egg white
6 Coupelles Cornets (page 65)
Frosted Grapes (page 97)

Place raisins, lemon juice and Amaretto in a small basin and leave to macerate for 1 hour.

Chop almonds into slivers and toast them. Finely chop the cherries, peel, ginger and pineapple, and fold them with 1 ounce (25g) toasted almonds and the raisins into the Soft Cheese Cream mixture. Chill 30 minutes.

Divide the mixture between 6 Coupelle Cornets. Serve with Frosted Grapes.

Crème à la Coeur

Six 2½in (6cm) portions

½ quantity Soft Cheese Cream recipe, omitting egg white and using curd cheese instead of cream cheese

To serve
6 Chocolate Shells*
4 ounces (100g) fraises des bois or raspberries

Line a small sieve with muslin or white kitchen paper and place over a basin. Make the Soft Cheese Cream mixture using the curd cheese instead of cream cheese. Place the mixture in the sieve and lightly smooth the surface. Loosely cover with a cloth and leave in a cool place overnight. Turn on to a plate and remove muslin.

Place Chocolate Shells on six small serving plates. Using a dessertspoon (10ml spoon), scoop out the mixture and place in the centre of each shell. Place fruit round the edge of each.

Pies, Tarts

The best pies and tarts have a thin lining of crisp, tasty pastry. Match the type to the filling: crisp unsweetened shortcrust for a sweet meringue-topped pie, for example, and flaky rich puff pastry with a moist filling for covered ones. Top pies with a variety of confections from chocolate curls to a delicious pastry lattice. Open tarts can show the splendour of the filling.

Shortcrust Pastry

This quickly made everyday pastry is the pride of pastrycooks. The fat is rubbed into the flour with cool fingertips or in a food processor. The texture is short and crisp and the type of fat used is important. A mixture of whipped cooking fat or lard for shortness and butter for flavour makes the best pastry.

Shortcrust Pastry

Four 4in (10cm) pies, tarts; 6 portions each

4 ounces (100g) plain white flour
1 ounce (25g) whipped cooking fat or lard
1 ounce (25g) butter
Cold water to mix

Place flour in a bowl or food processor and add the fats. Cut the fats in the flour with a knife, then rub in the flour with the fingertips or in the processor until the mixture looks like breadcrumbs.

Add about 4 teaspoons (4 × 5ml spoons) cold water and mix to a firm dough. Wrap in cling film and chill until required. Divide the rubbed-in mixture into four small basins and flavour three of them as opposite:

Flavourings
Sage
Spread fresh sage leaves on a baking sheet and place in the oven at 275°F, 140°C, Gas Mark 1, or in a microwave oven, until crisp. Crush the leaves.

Add 1 teaspoon (1 × 5ml spoon) leaves to the rubbed-in mixture before adding water.

Cheese
Add 1 ounce (25g) finely grated mature hard Cheddar cheese to the rubbed-in mixture before adding water.

Walnut
Add ½ ounce (15g) finely chopped walnuts to the rubbed-in mixture before adding water.

Quantities
Divide the flavouring ingredients proportionately – by a quarter or a half – to make smaller quantities of flavoured Shortcrust Pastry.

Alternatively, make the full quantities given above and freeze any pastry you do not use.

Previous pages, clockwise from left *Miniature (4in/ 10cm) Pecan Pie (opposite); Quick Lime Meringue Pie (page 41); Blueberry Tarts (page 45); Lemon Curd Tarts (page 48); Coconut Macaroon Tarts (page 49); Chocolate Marron Glacé Tarts (page 49); Chocolate Cheesecake (page 48); Morello Cherry Cheesecake (page 48).*

Curd and Currant Lattice Pie

One 4in (10cm) pie; 6 portions

¼ Shortcrust Pastry recipe, with sage flavour

Filling
1 small egg
4 ounces (100g) curd cheese
1 teaspoon (1 × 5ml spoon) caster sugar
½ ounce (15g) currants
½ teaspoon (1 × 2.5ml spoon) grated lemon rind
Beaten egg to glaze

Prepare a moderate oven at 375°F, 190°C, Gas Mark 5. Cut off one-third of the pastry and roll the larger piece to line a 4in (10cm) round 1¼in (3cm)-deep fluted pie tin. Roll the smaller piece to the size of the top and cut into thin strips.

Mix filling ingredients together and pour into lined pie tin. Cover with a lattice of pastry strips and attach the ends to the sides of the pie with the beaten egg. Brush all over with beaten egg.

Place on a baking sheet and bake 20 to 25 minutes until the filling is set. Serve cold cut into six portions.

Pecan Pie

One 4in (10cm) pie; 6 portions

¼ Shortcrust Pastry recipe

Filling
2 tablespoons (2 × 15ml spoons) dark corn syrup
1 ounce (25g) caster sugar
1 tablespoon (1 × 15ml spoon) melted butter
A few drops vanilla extract
2 ounces (50g) pecan halves

To serve
4 tablespoons (4 × 15ml spoons) whipped cream

Prepare a moderate oven at 375°F, 190°C, Gas Mark 5. Roll out pastry on a floured board and line a 4in (10cm) round 1¼in (3cm)-deep fluted pie tin. Press well into the base and the fluted side.

Beat egg and add the syrup, sugar, butter and vanilla. Place the pecans in the pastry case and pour the syrup mixture over. Place the pie tin on a baking sheet and bake for 30 minutes until the filling is set.

Serve cold cut into six portions with whipped cream.

Chocolate Meringue Pie

One 4in (10cm) pie; 6 portions

¼ Shortcrust Pastry recipe, with walnut flavour

Filling
2 ounces (50g) plain chocolate
1 tablespoon (1 × 15ml spoon) melted butter
1 egg yolk
1 tablespoon (1 × 15ml spoon) boiling water
1 tablespoon (1 × 15ml spoon) dark brown sugar
¼ teaspoon (1 × 1.25ml spoon) ground cinnamon

Topping
1 egg white
1 ounce (25g) moist brown sugar
A few Chocolate Curls*

Prepare a moderately hot oven at 375°F, 190°C, Gas Mark 5. Roll out pastry and line a 4in (10cm) ¾in (2cm)-deep fluted pie tin. Roll surplus pastry off the top; chill.

Melt chocolate and butter in a small basin over a saucepan of hot water or in a microwave oven. Remove from heat. Stir in egg yolk, boiling water, sugar and cinnamon. Pour into pastry case.

Bake 20 minutes until the pastry is browned and the filling is set. Reduce oven temperature to a cool setting of 275°F, 140°C, Gas Mark 1.

To make the topping, whisk egg white until stiff. Whisk in half the sugar and fold in the remainder. Pile or pipe on the chocolate mixture and dry out for ½ hour. Serve hot or cold cut into six wedges and decorated with Chocolate Curls.

Muesli and Honey Tart

One 4in (10cm) pie; 6 portions

¼ Shortcrust Pastry recipe, with cheese flavour

Filling
1 ounce (25g) muesli
1 teaspoon (1 × 5ml spoon) grated lemon rind
1 tablespoon (1 × 15ml spoon) lemon juice
5 tablespoons (5 × 15ml spoons) clear honey

Prepare a moderately hot oven at 400°F, 200°C, Gas Mark 6. Roll out the pastry thinly and line a 4in (10cm) round 1¼in (3cm)-deep fluted pie tin. Roll off excess pastry from the top.

Place muesli in the pastry case. Mix the lemon rind and juice with the honey and pour over.

Place pie tin on a baking sheet and bake in the oven for 20 minutes until the filling is set.

Puff Pastry

Layers of melt-in-the-mouth buttery pastry make a crisp contrast to moist fillings for pies and tarts. Seal the pastry well to prevent the filling boiling out at the high oven temperature that puff pastry needs.

Puff Pastry

18 portions

4 ounces (100g) butter
4 ounces (100g) plain flour
1 teaspoon (1 × 5ml spoon) lemon juice
3 tablespoons (3 × 15ml spoons) ice-cold water

Place butter on a plate and mash with a fork until softened. Divide into four portions. Put the flour into a small mixing bowl and rub one portion of the butter into the flour. Mix lemon juice and water and add all at once to the flour. Mix with a fork to a soft dough.

Turn out on to a floured board and knead lightly with the fingertips. Place on a plate, cover with cling film and leave in the refrigerator with the plate of butter to chill for 15 minutes.

Roll out pastry to an oblong 15 × 5in (38 × 12.5cm) and brush off surplus flour. Take a portion of butter, cut it into small pieces and cover the top two-thirds of the dough to within ¼in (6mm) of the edges. Fold bottom third up to cover the butter and fold top third over the folded dough. Press the edges with a rolling pin to seal. Turn the dough so that the folds are at the sides and flatten it lightly with the rolling pin. Repeat rolling and folding using another portion of butter cut into small pieces. Cover and chill for at least 20 minutes. Repeat with remaining portion of butter, then repeat the rolling and folding without adding any fat.

Cover pastry and chill for at least ½ hour before using to make the following recipes. The pastry can be wrapped and frozen at this stage, if preferred.

Omani Almond Pie

Six 2in (5cm) pies

⅓ Puff Pastry recipe

Filling
1 ounce (25g) ground almonds
1 ounce (25g) moist brown sugar
½ teaspoon (1 × 2.5ml spoon) rose water
Pinch of ground cardamom
Beaten egg to moisten

To serve
6 tablespoons (6 × 15ml spoons) apricot purée

Roll the pastry very thinly and cut out six circles with a 2in (5cm) plain cutter and the same number with a 2½in (6cm) plain cutter.

Mix the almonds, sugar, rose water, cardamom, and 1 teaspoon (1 × 5ml spoon) egg in a small bowl. Spoon the mixture on to the 2in (5cm) circles, then brush the edges with water. Score the remaining circles with the point of a knife from centre to edge in a spiral, then cover each almond mound and seal the edges well. Brush with egg, adding a few drops of water, if necessary.

Prepare a hot oven at 425°7F, 220°C, Gas Mark 7.

Place pies on a baking sheet and bake near the top of the oven for about 10 minutes until risen and golden brown.

Serve with apricot purée.

Marron Glacé Pie

Six 2in (5cm) pies

⅓ Puff Pastry recipe

Filling
2 marrons glacés, each cut into 3 pieces

For serving
¼ pint (150ml) Custard Sauce*

Make as for Omani Almond Pie replacing the almond filling with a piece of marron glacé in each.
Serve with Custard Sauce.

Left, from top *Spiced Apple Crescent (page 40); Omani Almond Pie (above); 7 × 4in (18 × 10cm) Tarte Française (page 40); Spiced Apple Crescent (page 40).*

Cherry and Cheese Pie

Six 2in (5cm) pies

1/3 Puff Pastry recipe (page 39)

Filling
2 maraschino cocktail cherries
1 ounce (25g) cream cheese
1 teaspoon (1 × 5ml spoon) maraschino-flavoured
* syrup from the jar*
1 teaspoon (1 × 5ml spoon) beaten egg

Roll out pastry and cut six 2in (5cm) circles and six 2½in (6cm) circles.

Chop the cherries finely and mix with the cream cheese, syrup and egg. Place a little filling in the centres of the 2in (5cm) circles, then finish as for Omani Almond Pie (page 39).

Spiced Apple Crescents

Eight 2in (5cm) crescents

1 small cooking apple
1 tablespoon (1 × 15ml spoon) granulated sugar
½ teaspoon (1 × 2.5ml spoon) ground cinnamon
1/3 Puff Pastry recipe (page 39)
1 egg white, lightly beaten

Prepare a hot oven at 425°F, 220°C, Gas Mark 7.

Peel the apple, cut into eight wedges and remove the core. Mix sugar and cinnamon on a plate; coat the apple wedges.

Roll out the pastry thinly and cut out circles about 3in (7cm) in diameter, ½in (1.25cm) bigger than the size of the apple wedges. Brush round the edges with water and place an apple wedge in each centre. Fold over the pastry to enclose, and seal each one well. Cut up the edges with a knife and flute with the fingers. Brush one side of each crescent with egg white and invert on to the cinnamon sugar. Place on a wetted baking sheet, chill 5 minutes, then bake in the oven until risen and golden brown, about 15 minutes.

Tarte Française

One 7 × 4in (18 × 10cm) tart; 6 portions

1/3 Puff Pastry recipe (page 39)
Beaten egg to glaze
2 tablespoons (2 × 15ml spoons) Apricot Glaze*

Filling
1 ounce (25g) fraises des bois or wild strawberries
3 green grapes
10 mandarin orange segments from a can, drained
* and dried*
2 to 3 strawberries, sliced

To serve
6 tablespoons (6 × 15ml spoons) brandy-flavoured
* whipped cream*

Roll the pastry and trim to an oblong, 7 × 4in (18 × 10cm) and about ¼in (6mm) thick. Fold the pastry in half lengthways and cut round the folded pastry ½in (1.25cm) away from the edge. Carefully open out each piece. Roll the newly cut-out central oblong and trim to the original size 7 × 4in (18 × 10cm). Brush the rim of the oblong with water and gently press the border on top, trimming to shape, if necessary. Cut into the edges with a knife. Mark the border in a criss-cross design with a knife and prick the inside.

Brush the pastry case with beaten egg, then place on a baking sheet and chill for about 5 minutes.

Prepare a hot oven at 425°F, 220°C, Gas Mark 7.

Bake the pastry case for about 10 minutes until risen and golden brown.

Meanwhile, heat Apricot Glaze gently in a small saucepan or in a microwave oven. Remove pastry from the oven and brush with some of the glaze. Leave until cold.

Arrange fruit in rows in the pastry case and brush with Apricot Glaze. Serve with brandy-flavoured whipped cream.

Freezing Puff Pastry
Cut the Puff Pastry into thirds before freezing for these recipes.
Alternatively, make up the pies, freeze them on the baking sheets after chilling, then pack in boxes and seal.
Cook from frozen, allowing about 4 minutes extra cooking time.

Crumb Crust

This versatile crust can be used baked or unbaked, as a base or topping for flans, cheesecakes and tarts. It freezes well, both cooked and uncooked.

Golden Crumb Crust

Eight 4in (10cm) pie bases; 32 portions

4 ounces (100g) digestive biscuits
1 tablespoon (1 × 15ml spoon) golden syrup
2 ounces (50g) butter

Crush the biscuits in a paper bag with a rolling pin, or in a food processor. Melt the golden syrup and butter in a small saucepan over a low heat.

Chocolate
Add 2 ounces (50g) melted plain chocolate.

Quantities
Divide the flavouring ingredients proportionately – by a quarter or a half – to make smaller quantities of flavoured Golden Crumb Crusts. Alternatively, make the full quantities and freeze any you do not use.

Quick Lime Meringue Pie

Two 4in (10cm) pies; 8 portions

¼ Golden Crumb Crust recipe

Filling
1 7-ounce (197g) can sweetened condensed milk
Grated rind and juice of 1 lime
1 egg, separated
3 tablespoons (3 × 15ml spoons) caster sugar
8 pieces candied lime or lime slices

Prepare a moderate oven at 350°F, 180°C, Gas Mark 4. Press the crumb crust into two 4in (10cm) loose-bottomed flan rings (or line with foil if the base is solid). Mix milk, lime rind and juice and the egg yolk, and divide between the flan cases.

Whisk egg white until stiff. Whisk in one tablespoon of sugar and fold in another tablespoon of sugar. Pile into a piping bag fitted with a star tube and pipe whirls of meringue over the filling. Sprinkle with remaining tablespoon of sugar.

Bake for about 5 minutes until pale golden brown. Decorate with the candied lime or lime slices.

Apricot Pies

Two 4in (10cm) pies; 8 portions

4 ounces (100g) dried apricots
¼ pint (125ml) sweet white vermouth
¼ pint (125ml) water
4 ounces (100g) prepared cooking apple
4 ounces (100g) sugar
½ Golden Crumb Crust
2 ounces (50g) blanched almonds
4 tablespoons (4 × 15ml spoons) whipped cream

Soak the apricots in the vermouth and water overnight. Place in a medium saucepan and add the apple; cook over a low heat until the fruit is soft and the liquid reduced. Add the sugar and cook, stirring frequently, until the mixture is thick.

Spread two-thirds of the crumb crust mixture into two 4 × 2¼in (10 × 6cm) miniature bread tins. Cover with the apricot mixture then top with the remaining crumbs. Decorate with the almonds. Allow to cool, then chill.

Cut into bars and serve with whipped cream.

Banana Cream Pie

One 4in (10cm) pie; 4 portions

¼ Golden Crumb Crust with chocolate flavour
1 small banana
1 teaspoon (1 × 5ml spoon) lemon juice
2 squares chocolate, melted
⅛ pint (65ml) double cream
1 tablespoon (1 × 15ml spoon) Tia Maria
½ teaspoon (1 × 2.5ml spoon) cocoa powder
2 pistachio nuts, chopped

Line a 4in (10cm) pie tin with foil and press crumb crust mixture over base and sides.

Slice the banana and coat in lemon juice to prevent browning. Dip half the slices into melted chocolate and leave on foil to set. Spread remaining chocolate over base of pie and cover with remaining banana slices.

Whip cream with Tia Maria and pipe over banana top. Dust with cocoa powder and decorate with the chocolate banana pieces and nuts.

Pâte Sucrée

This rich sweet dough is the classic French pastry for sweet flans. It is very tender, but easy to handle if kept chilled. Use it for a variety of tarts and flans or flavour and layer it to make delicious tortes. It freezes well both cooked and raw.

Pâte Sucrée

12 to 16 portions

3 ounces (75g) butter
2 ounces (50g) caster sugar
1 egg yolk
5 ounces (125g) plain flour

Cream the butter and sugar together, add egg yolk then flour and mix to a soft dough then knead until smooth. Alternatively, place all the ingredients in a food processor and run the machine until a dough is formed.

Wrap the dough in cling film and chill for at least ½ hour. Use for the following recipes, or freeze at this stage, if desired.

Flavourings

Chocolate
Knead 1 tablespoon (1 × 15ml spoon) cocoa into the pastry with ½ teaspoon (1 × 2.5ml spoon) milk.

Ginger
Add 2 teaspoons (2 × 5ml spoons) ground ginger.

Hazelnut
Add 1 ounce (25g) finely chopped Toasted Hazelnuts*.

Quantities

Divide the flavouring ingredients proportionately – by a quarter or a half – to make smaller quantities of flavoured Pâte Sucrée.

Alternatively, make the full quantities and freeze any pastry you do not use.

Normandy Flan

One 4in (10cm) pie; 4 portions

¼ Pâte Sucrée

Filling
8 ounces (200g) prepared cooking apples
1 teaspoon (1 × 5ml spoon) lemon juice
1 teaspoon (1 × 5ml spoon) caster sugar
1 knob of butter
¼ teaspoon (½ × 2.5ml spoon) ground cinnamon
½ teaspoon (1 × 2.5ml spoon) grated lemon rind
2 teaspoons (2 × 5ml spoons) apricot jam
2 teaspoons (2 × 5ml spoons) Calvados

Glaze
1 tablespoon (1 × 15ml spoon) apricot jam
1 tablespoon (1 × 15ml spoon) Calvados
1 tablespoon (1 × 15ml spoon) caster sugar

Prepare a moderate oven at 375°F, 190°C, Gas Mark 5. Roll out the pastry and line a 4in (10cm) loose-based fluted flan tin; chill.

Cut apples into quarters. Remove the core from one apple, but not the skin, and slice finely. Place on a plate, brush with lemon juice and sprinkle with sugar.

Peel and core the remaining apple and place in a small saucepan with the butter, cinnamon, lemon rind and jam. Stir over a low heat until the butter has melted, then cover and cook slowly until pulpy.

Press through a sieve, cool, add the Calvados and spoon into the pastry case, spreading it out. Arrange the sugared apple slices, overlapping, on top of the purée and bake for 20 to 25 minutes until the pastry is golden brown.

Meanwhile make the glaze. Place the jam, Calvados and sugar in a small saucepan and stir over a low heat until the mixture is thick and coats the back of the spoon.

Remove the flan from the oven and brush the glaze over the apples.

Right, clockwise from top *Selection of Frangipane Tartlets: Cherry Ripe (page 44); 2in (5cm) Chocolate Ginger (page 45); Strawberry (page 44); Walnut Coffee (page 45); Peach and Cream (page 44).*

Frangipane Tartlet Bases

Six 2in (5cm) tartlet bases

½ chocolate-flavoured Pâte Sucrée (page 42)

Frangipane
2 ounces (50g) butter
2 ounces (50g) caster sugar
1 egg
2 ounces (50g) ground almonds
1 tablespoon (1 × 15ml spoon) flour
A few drops almond extract
1 tablespoon (1 × 15ml spoon) kirsch

Place various-shaped petits fours moulds together on the table. Roll out the pastry and lift over the rolling pin to cover the moulds. Roll lightly over the top to cut off the pastry. Press the dough gently into each mould taking care to avoid stretching it. Chill the pastry.

Meanwhile make the frangipane. Cream butter and sugar together, gradually beating in the egg, then the almonds, flour, almond extract and kirsch.

Fit a piping bag with a ¼in (6mm) plain tube and half fill the tartlet cases with frangipane. If cooking is required at this stage, prepare a moderate oven at 325°F, 160°C, Gas Mark 3 and bake until the frangipane is set and browned, 20-25 minutes.

Ginger-flavoured Tartlet Cases: ½ ginger-flavoured Pâte Sucrée (page 42) makes six 2in (5cm) tartlets.

Hazelnut-flavoured Tartlet Cases: ½ hazelnut-flavoured Pâte Sucrée (page 42) makes six 2in (5cm) tartlets.

Strawberry Tartlets

Six 2in (5cm) tartlets

1 tablespoon (1 × 15ml spoon) Apricot Glaze*
1 teaspoon (1 × 5ml spoon) brandy
6 cooked hazelnut-flavoured Frangipane Tartlet
  Bases (above)
6 strawberries, sliced
4 tablespoons (4 × 15ml spoons) whipped cream
1 teaspoon (1 × 5ml spoon) chopped pistachio nuts

Heat the Apricot Glaze with the brandy gently in a cup in a small saucepan or microwave oven, then generously brush it over the frangipane. Slice and arrange strawberries on top of each tartlet and brush with more glaze. Pipe a swirl of cream on each and decorate with chopped pistachio nuts.

Peach and Cream Tartlets

Six 2in (5cm) tartlets

2 tablespoons (2 × 15ml spoons) Chantilly Cream
  (page 122)
1 teaspoon (1 × 5ml spoon) peach purée
Orange food colouring
2 tablespoons (2 × 15ml spoons) Praline Cream
  (page 122)
6 cooked hazelnut-flavoured Frangipane Tartlet
  Bases (left)
6 fresh peach slices, cut small
Flaked Almonds

Fit a nylon piping bag with a small star tube.

Mix, in a small bowl, the Chantilly Cream with peach purée and a drop of orange food colouring. Place the Praline Cream down one side of the piping bag and the peach cream down the other side. Place a peach slice on each tartlet, pipe on the creams and decorate with almonds.

Cherry Ripe Tartlet

Six 2in (5cm) tartlets

1½ tablespoons (1½ × 15ml spoons)
  Apricot Glaze*
6 cooked chocolate-flavoured Frangipane Tartlet
  Bases (top left)
2 tablespoons (2 × 15ml spoons) double cream
1 teaspoon (1 × 5ml spoon) cherry brandy
6 preserved cherries with stems

Heat the Apricot Glaze gently in a small saucepan, then brush it over the Frangipane Tartlets. Leave to cool.

Whip the cream with the cherry brandy and pipe whirls on the tarts. Arrange the cherries on top.

Blueberry Tarts

Twelve 2½in (6cm) tarts

¼ Pâte Sucrée (page 42)
2 ounces blueberries (or blackcurrants)
1 teaspoon (1 × 5ml spoon) caster sugar
1 teaspoon (1 × 5ml spoon) cornflour
½ teaspoon (1 × 2.5ml spoon) grated lemon rind
2 tablespoons (2 × 15ml spoons) redcurrant jelly
12 Meringue Stars (page 125)

Prepare a moderate oven at 375°F, 190°C, Gas Mark 5. Roll out the pastry fairly thickly and cut out twelve 1½in (6cm) circles. Press into tartlet tins, making the bases thinner.

Mix the blueberries, sugar, cornflour and lemon rind; divide between the tins. Bake in the centre of the oven about 25 minutes until the pastry is golden brown. Cool 5 minutes, then remove from the tins and brush the fruit with redcurrant jelly. Serve topped with tiny Meringue Stars.

Linzertorte

Six 1¾in (4.5cm) tartlets

Pinch of ground cinnamon
1 ounce (25g) ground almonds
1 teaspoon (1 × 5ml spoon) grated lemon rind
¼ Pâte Sucrée (page 42)

Filling
2 ounces (50g) raspberries
1 ounce (25g) caster sugar
1 beaten egg
1½ tablespoons (1½ × 15ml spoons) raspberry
  jelly to glaze
4 tablespoons (4 × 15ml spoons) whipped cream
  for serving

Prepare a moderate oven at 375°F, 190°C, Gas Mark 5. Knead the cinnamon, almonds and lemon rind into the pastry, then chill. Cook the raspberries and sugar together until pulpy, then cool.

Divide the pastry into six pieces and press four pieces into deep 2in (5cm) tartlet tins to line the bases and sides. Roll out and cut the remainder into thin strips. Fill each lined tartlet with raspberry mixture and cover with a lattice of strips, first brushing them with beaten egg to secure.

Bake 20 minutes until golden brown, remove from oven and leave to cool five minutes.

Meanwhile gently melt the jelly in a small saucepan or in a microwave oven. Brush tartlets with the jelly. Serve with whipped cream.

Chocolate Ginger Tartlets

Six 2in (5cm) tartlets

4 small pieces stem ginger
6 uncooked ginger-flavoured Frangipane Tartlet
  Cases (far left)
1 Frangipane mixture (far left)
1 teaspoon (1 × 5ml spoon) Apricot Glaze*
2 tablespoons (2 × 15ml spoons) Chocolate Fudge
  Icing*
4 tablespoons (4 × 15ml spoons) whipped cream
1 teaspoon (1 × 5ml spoon) chopped pistachio nuts

Slice three pieces of stem ginger finely and line each tartlet case before piping in the frangipane.

Bake as directed, then brush with Apricot Glaze.

Cover with Chocolate Fudge Icing and leave to set. Pipe four shells of cream on each and decorate with remaining ginger and chopped pistachio nuts.

Walnut Coffee Tartlets

Six 2in (5cm) tartlets

1 ounce (25g) shelled walnuts
6 uncooked chocolate-flavoured Frangipane
  Tartlet Cases (far left)
1 Frangipane mixture (far left)
2 rounded tablespoons (2 × 15ml spoons) Rich
  Butter Cream*
2 teaspoons (2 × 5ml spoons) Tia Maria
Chocolate coffee beans, optional

Reserve six half walnuts for decoration, if desired, and divide the remainder between the tartlet cases before piping in the frangipane.

Bake as directed then chill.

Flavour the Rich Butter Cream by mixing in the Tia Maria, and pipe it over the frangipane. Decorate with half walnuts or chocolate coffee beans.

Ingredients, sauces, edible containers, etc that are asterisked in the recipes on these pages are given in detail on pages 147 to 156. For exact page numbers, refer to the index at the end of the book.

Biscuit Crust

This is a crisp, easily managed pastry that can be rolled very thinly. It is perfect for flans with deep or heavy fillings, makes a good baked cheesecake base and is meltingly crisp for tartlets. Biscuit Crust freezes well, both raw and cooked. Prick the base of a flan and brush it with egg white if you fill it before freezing.

Biscuit Crust Pastry

36 to 72 portions

4 ounces (100g) plain flour
1 ounce (25g) icing sugar
2½ ounces (65g) butter, softened
2 teaspoons (2 × 5ml spoons) chilled milk

Place half the flour with the sugar, butter and water in a medium bowl and beat together. Add remaining flour and mix to a firm dough.
  Wrap in cling film and chill for ½ hour.

Flavourings

Almond
Add 1 ounce (25g) ground almonds, 1 extra teaspoon (1 × 5ml spoon) water and a few drops of almond extract.

Orange or Lemon
Add 2 teaspoons (2 × 5ml spoons) finely grated rind.

Cinnamon
Add 1 teaspoon (1 × 5ml spoon) ground cinnamon.

> ### Quantities
> Divide the flavouring ingredients proportionately – by a quarter or a half – to make smaller quantities of flavoured Biscuit Crust Pastry.
>   Alternatively, make the full quantities given above and freeze any you do not use.

Smooth Cheesecake Pie

One 6in (15cm) pie; 18 portions

½ Biscuit Crust Pastry recipe

Filling

½lb (200g) medium-fat soft (curd) cheese
1 teaspoon (1 × 5ml spoon) each of lemon rind and juice
1 ounce (25g) melted butter
½ teaspoon (1 × 1.25ml spoon) vanilla extract
1 tablespoon (1 × 15ml spoon) cornflour
1 tablespoon (1 × 15ml spoon) natural yoghurt
1 egg white
1 ounce (25g) caster sugar

Prepare a moderate oven at 325°F, 170°C, Gas Mark 3. Roll out the pastry and line a 6in (15cm) loose-based round sponge tin (or line the tin with foil if it has a solid base). Bake for 10 minutes.
  Beat together the cheese, lemon rind and juice, butter, vanilla, cornflour and yoghurt. Whisk egg white until stiff then whisk in 2 teaspoons (2 × 5ml spoons) sugar. Beat remaining sugar into cheese mixture then fold in the meringue. Pour over the pastry base, then tap to level the surface.
  Bake in the centre of the oven for 15 minutes or until the cheesecake is set 1in (2.5cm) in from the sides. (If the cheesecake rises in the centre, the oven is too hot.) Leave to cool then chill overnight before serving.

> ### Alternative Cheesecake
> ½ Golden Crumb Crust recipe (page 41) can be used as a base for the cheesecakes, but do not pre-bake.

Right *Selection of 1in (2.5cm) Ripe Berry Tartlets: Strawberry, Raspberry, Blackberry.*

Chocolate Cheesecake

One 4 × 4in (10 × 10cm) or 4 × 2¼in (10 × 6cm) cheesecake; 6 portions

⅛ *Biscuit Crust Pastry (page 46)*
⅓ *Smooth Cheesecake Pie filling (page 46), omitting lemon rind and juice*
1 ounce (25g) plain dessert chocolate, melted
1 teaspoon (1 × 5ml spoon) dark rum

Decoration
11 mandarin orange segments
Apricot Glaze*

Set oven at 325°F, 170°C, Gas Mark 3.
   Roll out pastry and line a 4 × 4in (10 × 10cm) tin or a miniature bread tin 4 × 2¼in (10 × 6cm). Bake for 7 to 10 minutes.
   Beat chocolate and rum into the cheesecake mixture before adding the egg white. Pour into the pastry case and bake for 20 minutes. Decorate with orange segments brushed with Apricot Glaze.

Lemon Curd Tarts

Six 1¾in (4cm) tarts

¼ *orange-flavoured Biscuit Crust Pastry recipe (page 46), used to line six 1¾in (4cm) tart tins*

Filling
1 tablespoon (1 × 15ml spoon) butter, melted
1 tablespoon (1 × 15ml spoon) caster sugar
1 tablespoon (1 × 15ml spoon) beaten egg
2 tablespoons (2 × 15ml spoons) ground almonds
Grated rind and juice of 1 small lemon

Decoration
Slices from a small lemon
1 tablespoon (1 × 15ml spoon) sugar

Prepare a moderately hot oven at 400°F, 200°C, Gas Mark 6.
   Cream butter and sugar and beat in the egg, almonds and lemon. Divide between the tarts and bake until the filling is set, about 10 minutes.
   Place the lemon slices in a small saucepan, cover with water, bring to the boil and simmer for about 5 minutes until tender. Gently stir in the sugar, then cook uncovered until the water has nearly evaporated and the slices are shiny. Cool on non-stick baking parchment.
   Brush each tartlet with the lemon syrup and arrange the lemon slices, cut into wedges, on top.

Morello Cherry Cheesecake

One 6in (15cm) cheesecake; 18 portions

⅛ *Biscuit Crust Pastry (page 46)*
⅓ *Smooth Cheesecake Pie filling (page 46)*
1 teaspoon (1 × 5ml spoon) grated orange rind

Topping
4 ounces (100g) morello cherries
1 ounce (25g) caster sugar
1 tablespoon (1 × 15ml spoon) cherry brandy
½ teaspoon (1 × 2.5ml spoon) arrowroot

Follow the Smooth Cheesecake Pie recipe, but add the orange rind to the filling. Cook as directed.
   Remove the stones and cook the cherries gently in a small saucepan with 2 tablespoons (2 × 15ml spoons) water and the sugar. Add the cherry brandy and arrowroot, stir and cook until thickened and clear.
   Arrange over the chilled cheesecake and leave to set.

Sicilian Cheesecake

One 4 × 4in (10 × 10cm) or 4 × 2¼in (10 × 6cm) cheesecake; 6 portions

⅛ *Biscuit Crust Pastry (page 46)*
1 ounce (25g) glacé fruits
1 teaspoon (1 × 5ml spoon) Strega liqueur
⅓ *Smooth Cheesecake Pie filling (page 46)*
1 ounce (25g) dessert chocolate
2 squares white chocolate for decoration

Prepare oven and pastry case as for Chocolate Cheesecake.
   Chop the fruits and marinate in Strega overnight then mix into the cheesecake filling. Chop the dark chocolate and add half to the cheesecake mixture. Pour into the pastry case and bake for 20 minutes. Cool slowly, then chill.
   Melt the remaining dessert chocolate and the white chocolate in small separate bowls over hot water or in a microwave oven. Spread the dark chocolate over the cheesecake, then swirl the white chocolate in with it.

Ripe Berry Tartlets

Eighteen 1in (2.5cm) tarts

¼ almond-flavoured Biscuit Crust Pastry recipe (page 46), used to line 18 petits fours tins

Filling
1 ounce (25g) softened butter
1 ounce (25g) caster sugar
3½ ounces (100g) cream cheese
1 tablespoon (1 × 15ml spoon) Drambuie liqueur
1 tablespoon (1 × 15ml spoon) Grand Marnier
1 tablespoon (1 × 15ml spoon) apricot brandy
3 tablespoons (3 × 15ml spoons) raspberry or
*   redcurrant jelly*
1 tablespoon (1 × 15ml spoon) kirsch
6 blackberries
6 strawberries
6 raspberries
4 tablespoons (4 × 15ml spoons) Chantilly Cream
*   (page 122)*

Prepare a moderately hot oven at 400°F, 200°C, Gas Mark 6.

Prick the pastry with a fork, chill 10 minutes, then bake about 6 minutes until pale golden brown. Cool in the tins, then remove.

Cream the butter and sugar together, beat in the cream cheese, then divide between three small basins or cups and beat a liqueur into each.

Gently heat the raspberry or redcurrant jelly in a small saucepan with the kirsch and brush inside each tartlet case. Divide the flavoured cream cheese between the pastry cases, keeping the flavours separate. Place a blackberry with the Drambuie cheese, a strawberry with the Grand Marnier cheese and a raspberry with the apricot brandy cheese. Brush each with the remaining jelly. Serve with Chantilly Cream.

Coconut Macaroon Tarts

Six 1¾in (4cm) tarts

¼ orange-flavoured Biscuit Crust Pastry recipe (page 46), used to line six 1¾in (4cm) tart tins

Filling
1 tablespoon (1 × 15ml spoon) butter
1 tablespoon (1 × 15ml spoon) caster sugar
1 tablespoon (1 × 15ml spoon) egg white
1 ounce (25g) desiccated coconut
2 glacé cherries, chopped
1 tablespoon (1 × 15ml spoon) raspberry jam

Prepare a moderately hot oven at 400°F, 200°C, Gas Mark 6.

Cream together the butter and sugar and beat in the egg white, then fold in the coconut and cherries. Place a little jam in each tart case and divide the coconut mixture between the tarts.

Bake in the centre of the oven until golden brown – about 15 minutes.

Chocolate Marron Glacé Tarts

Six 2½in (6cm) tarts

¼ Biscuit Crust Pastry recipe (page 46), flavoured with cinnamon, used to line six 2½in (6cm) tart tins

Filling
1 ounce (25g) plain chocolate, chopped
1 fluid ounce (25ml) whipping cream
2 ounces (50g) unsweetened chestnut purée
1 teaspoon (1 × 5ml spoon) icing sugar
2 teaspoons (2 × 5ml spoons) brandy
1 marron glacé, chopped
6 white Chocolate Leaves*, optional

Prepare a moderately hot oven at 400°F, 200°C, Gas Mark 6. Prick the tarts with a fork then bake until golden brown, about 15 minutes. Leave to cool then remove from the tins.

To make the filling, heat the chocolate and cream in a small saucepan, or in a basin in a microwave oven, until smooth; cool. Beat in the chestnut purée, icing sugar and brandy then place the mixture in a piping bag fitted with a small star tube. Pipe a circle in each tart and top each with a piece of marron glacé. Decorate with a white Chocolate Leaf, optional.

Pastries

*Tiny decorative pastries, made from special doughs, can be filled with
liqueur-laced creams, custards, fruits and marzipan and topped with icings,
caramel or a shower of icing sugar.*

Layered and Shaped Pastries

Several of these recipes use the puff pastry described in Pies, Tarts – combined
with other ingredients to create tiny, light-as-air confections. Recipes with filo
pastry are also included.

Raspberry Millefeuilles

One 7 × 3in (18 × 7.5cm) bar; 6 portions

¼ quantity Puff Pastry recipe (page 39)
6 tablespoons (6 × 15ml spoons) raspberry jam
½ quantity kirsch-flavoured Diplomat Cream*
3 ounces (75g) raspberries
2 tablespoons (2 × 15ml spoons) icing sugar

Prepare a hot oven at 425°F, 220°C, Gas Mark 7.
   Roll the pastry and trim to an oblong 7 × 6in (18
× 15cm). Cut in half to make two 3 × 7in (18cm)
strips and place on a wetted baking sheet. Cook 7 to
10 minutes until risen and browned. Split through
the thickness of each and dry out in the oven for
2 minutes; cool, then trim the edges.
   Assemble the layers on a serving dish. Spread half
the jam and half the Diplomat Cream on the bottom
pastry layer. Cover with pastry then spread with
raspberries, another layer of pastry, the remaining
jam and Diplomat Cream and the final layer of
pastry.
   Dredge thickly with icing sugar. Heat a skewer
and press into the sugar to caramelize. Repeat,
making a diamond design. Cut in six slices to serve.

Previous pages, clockwise from left *Plate of Danish
Pastries (all on page 57): Star surrounded by Tivoli with
Vanilla Cream filling, Pinwheel, Spandauer, Tivoli with
Apple and Raisin filling and 1½in (3.5cm) Pinwheel;
Almond Cornets (opposite); Baklavas (above right); Fruit
Strudel (opposite); Raspberry Millefeuilles (above).*

Baklava

Sixty-four 1in (2.5cm) baklavas

Eleven 12 × 10in (30 × 25cm) sheets filo pastry
5 ounces (125g) clarified butter or ghee

Filling
4 ounces (100g) mixed chopped nuts
2 ounces (50g) caster sugar
1 teaspoon (1 × 5ml spoon) ground cinnamon
1 tablespoon (1 × 15ml spoon) rose water

Syrup
4 ounces (100g) sugar
Pared rind and juice of 1 lemon
2 tablespoons (2 × 15ml spoons) honey
1 vanilla pod
1 tablespoon (1 × 15ml spoon) rose water

Prepare a moderate oven at 350°F, 180°C, Gas Mark
4. Keep the pastry covered with a damp cloth. Brush
a 12 × 10 × 2in (30 × 25 × 5cm) oblong baking tin
with butter or ghee. Spread a sheet of pastry over,
then brush with butter or ghee. Repeat with three
more layers of pastry.
   Mix the nuts, sugar and cinnamon and sprinkle
one-third over. Cover with another layer of pastry,
then butter. Repeat twice more with the remaining
filling and two more sheets of pastry.
   Add four more sheets of pastry, brushing
between each layer with butter. Cut in 1in (2.5cm)
strips down the length of the tin and across
diagonally to form diamond shapes. Sprinkle with
rose water. Bake for 35 minutes until golden brown.
   Meanwhile, place the syrup ingredients with
¼ pint (125ml) water in a small saucepan and
simmer 5 minutes. Strain over the hot pastry and
leave to cool in the tin.

Almond Cornets

Six 2in (5cm) cornets

¼ quantity Puff Pastry recipe (page 39)
2 tablespoons (2 × 15ml spoons) granulated sugar
2 ounces (50g) dessert chocolate, melted

Filling
1 ounce (25g) butter
1 ounce (25g) caster sugar
1 tablespoon (1 × 15ml spoon) Strega liqueur
1 ounce (25g) full-fat soft cheese
1 teaspoon (1 × 5ml spoon) grated orange
  rind
1 ounce (25g) ground almonds
2 drops almond extract
Chocolate Flakes*

Prepare a hot oven at 425°F, 220°C, Gas Mark 7.

Roll out the pastry and trim to a 12 × 4in (30 × 10cm) oblong. Cut in six long strips. Brush with water then roll round cream horn tins, first placing the point of the tin underneath the end of the strip and rolling the strip on with the wetted side of the pastry outside. Trim the end of the strip then dip the opposite side in sugar. Place sugar-side up on a wetted baking sheet and bake 5 to 7 minutes until golden brown; cool. Spread the inside of each cornet with melted chocolate.

Cream butter and sugar and beat in the liqueur. Divide into two small bowls and add the soft cheese and orange rind to one and the ground almonds and almond extract to the other. Place both mixtures in piping bags and pipe first the almond mixture, then the cheese mixture into the cornets. Decorate with Chocolate Flakes.

Fruit Strudels

Two 6in (15cm) strudels; 6 portions each

Two large 20 × 12in (50 × 30cm) sheets filo, fila or
  strudel pastry leaves

Filling
5 ounces (125g) butter, melted
5 ounces (125g) fresh breadcrumbs
2 ounces (50g) demerara sugar
1 ounce (25g) blanched shredded almonds
3 ounces (75g) prepared sliced apple
1 ounce (25g) raisins
4 ounces (100g) halved apricots, chopped
3 tablespoons (3 × 15ml spoons) icing sugar
6 fluid ounces (150ml) soured cream

Prepare a moderate oven at 375°F, 190°C, Gas Mark 5. Wring out a tea-towel in warm water and place on the table. Cut each sheet of pastry in half to make four 10 × 12in (25 × 30cm) sheets. Place one on the tea-towel and cover the others with a damp cloth. Mix 2 ounces (50g) of the butter with the breadcrumbs. Mix half the sugar and almonds with the apple and raisins. Finally, mix the remaining sugar and almonds with the apricots.

Brush the single sheet of pastry with melted butter and cover with one more sheet of pastry and butter. Spread half the crumb mixture over, then the apple filling over half, leaving a 1in (2.5cm) border all round. Fold in the border then roll up, using the cloth. Place seam-side down on a baking sheet and brush with more butter. Repeat with the apricot filling. Bake for ½ hour until the pastry is golden brown. Dredge with icing sugar, and serve warm or cold with soured cream.

Choux Pastry

'Choux' is French for cabbage and describes the way a ball of this pastry trebles
in size when baked and bursts open – like a cabbage.

Choux Pastry

Sixty 2½in (6cm) éclairs or about 36 profiteroles

2½ ounces (65g) plain flour
¼ pint (125ml) water
2 ounces (50g) butter
2 eggs, beaten

Prepare a moderately hot oven at 400°F, 200°C, Gas Mark 6. Grease a baking sheet and brush with water.

Sift flour on to a plate and place in the oven for 5 minutes then remove and sift on to a sheet of greaseproof paper.

Place water and butter in a small saucepan and bring slowly to boil. Remove from the heat, immediately add the flour all at once and beat well until a smooth ball is formed. Leave to cool, beating occasionally. Beat in the eggs a little at a time then use for any of the following recipes.

Chocolate Orange Éclairs

Fifteen 2½in (6cm) éclairs

¼ quantity Choux Pastry (page 53)

Filling
2 tablespoons (2 × 15ml spoons) Chantilly Cream
*   (page 122)*
1 teaspoon (1 × 5ml spoon) grated orange rind
1 teaspoon (1 × 5ml spoon) orange liqueur

Topping
1 ounce (25g) dessert chocolate
½ teaspoon (1 × 2.5ml spoon) sunflower oil

Fit a nylon piping bag with a ⅜in (1cm) plain tube and fill with Choux Pastry. Pipe fifteen 2½in (6cm) lengths on to the baking sheet. Bake for 25 to 30 minutes until risen and golden brown and crisp.

Remove from the oven and slit down one side to allow the steam to escape. Leave to cool.

For the filling, mix the Chantilly Cream, orange rind and liqueur. Pipe cream into éclairs. Break up the chocolate and melt it in a basin over a saucepan of hot water. Mix in the oil, then dip the tops of the éclairs into the chocolate and leave to set.

Rainbow Profiteroles

Thirty-six ⅜in (1cm) profiteroles; 6 portions

¼ quantity Choux Pastry (page 53)
4 fluid ounces (100ml) double cream
½ teaspoon (1 × 2.5ml spoon) rose water
2 ounces (50g) white chocolate
Yellow, pink and lilac paste food
*   colouring*
2 fluid ounces (50ml) Bailey's Cream Liqueur

Place the Choux Pastry in a nylon piping bag fitted with a small ⅜in (1cm) plain piping tube and pipe small balls on a greased baking sheet. Bake for 15 minutes until risen and golden. Cool on a wire rack.

Whip 2 fluid ounces (50ml) of the cream with the rose water and place in a nylon piping bag fitted with a small plain tube. Pierce the side of each pastry ball with a skewer and pipe cream in each.

Melt the chocolate in a cup over a saucepan of boiling water, or in a microwave oven. Dip six balls in the chocolate and leave to set. Add a few specks of yellow colouring to the chocolate and dip six more balls. Repeat with pink and lilac colouring, then more pink and lilac to make a raspberry colour. Mix the remaining cream with the liqueur and serve with the profiteroles.

St Honoré Puffs

Six 2in (5cm) puffs

¼ quantity Choux Pastry (page 53)
¼ quantity Biscuit Crust Pastry (page 46)
1 tablespoon (1 × 15ml spoon) beaten egg
6 tablespoons (6 × 15ml spoons) whipped cream
2 teaspoons (2 × 5ml spoons) Amaretto liqueur
3 ounces (75g) caster sugar
6 Chocolate Leaves*

Place the Choux Pastry in a nylon piping bag fitted with a ⅜in (1cm) star tube.

Roll out the Biscuit Crust Pastry and cut six 2in (5cm) circles. Place on a baking sheet and brush with beaten egg. Pipe a ring of Choux Pastry on each and six stars on the baking sheet. Brush with egg then bake for 12 to 15 minutes until golden brown. Cool then cut the Choux Pastry circles in half horizontally.

Mix the cream and liqueur and put in a piping bag fitted with a star tube. Pipe a ring of cream in each base and reserve remaining cream.

Place the caster sugar in a small saucepan and heat slowly until the sugar melts and turns golden brown. Dip the tops of the rings and the small stars into the caramel to coat, spearing them on a skewer. Replace the tops then pipe a star of cream in the centre of each, if desired. Decorate with Chocolate Leaves.

Praline Rings

Six 2½in (6cm) rings

¼ quantity Choux Pastry (page 53)
6 tablespoons (6 × 15ml spoons) Praline Cream
*   (page 122)*
2 teaspoons (2 × 5ml spoons) icing sugar

Prepare a hot oven at 400°F, 200°C, Gas Mark 6. Grease a baking sheet then sprinkle water over.

Place the pastry in a nylon piping bag fitted with a small star tube and pipe 2½in (6cm) rings on the baking sheet. Bake for 15 minutes until risen and golden brown.

Cool, split and fill with the Praline Cream then thickly dredge with icing sugar.

Right, from top *Selection of Choux Pastries (all on this page): Rainbow Profiteroles; St Honoré Puff; 2½in (6cm) Chocolate Orange Éclairs; Praline Ring.*

Danish Pastries

These buttery flaky pastries originated in Copenhagen when Austrian pastry chefs demonstrated their method of folding butter into dough and Danes took the method a stage further and made it into a variety of attractive shapes, adding moist and tasty fillings. It is worthwhile making a large quantity of dough at a time; it is easy to handle and freezes well.

Danish Pastries

Thirty-two 2 × 2in (5 × 5cm) pastries

Yeast Liquid
1 teaspoon (1 × 5ml spoon) caster sugar
5 tablespoons (5 × 15ml spoons) hand-hot water
2 teaspoons (2 × 5ml spoons) dried yeast

Dough
8 ounces (200g) plain flour
½ teaspoon (1 × 2.5ml spoon) salt
1 ounce (25g) lard
1 tablespoon (1 × 15ml spoon) caster sugar
1 egg, beaten
5 ounces (125g) butter

Egg Glaze
1 egg yolk, beaten
1 teaspoon (1 × 5ml spoon) caster sugar
1 tablespoon (1 × 15ml spoon) water

Dissolve sugar in the water in a small basin. Sprinkle on yeast, then leave in a warm place until frothy, about 10 minutes.

Place flour and salt in a bowl. Add lard, cut into small pieces, and rub in with the fingertips. Add 1 level tablespoon (1 × 15ml spoon) caster sugar, beaten egg and yeast liquid, and mix with a fork to form a soft dough. Turn out on to a floured board and knead lightly until smooth. Wrap in greased polythene and chill for 10 minutes.

Work the butter on a plate with a round-ended knife until soft (do not melt). Roll out dough to a 10in (25cm) square. Spread butter in an oblong 9 × 5in (23 × 12cm) in the centre of the dough, 2½in (7cm) from each end. Fold the two unbuttered ends of dough over, so that they just overlap each other in the centre. Press edges with a rolling pin, to seal.

Turn dough and roll out to an oblong about 15 × 5in (38 × 12cm). Fold dough, bringing top third over centre portion, then cover with lower third. Lift on to a plate, cover with foil or greased polythene and leave in the refrigerator for at least 10 minutes (in hot weather, leave for ½ hour, or until butter is very firm). Repeat rolling, folding and resting the dough twice more. Chill. Freeze if not required at once.

Shape and fill pastries as described in the following recipes.

For the glaze, beat egg yolk, sugar and a little water together and brush the pastries with the glaze. Place on a baking sheet and leave in a slightly warm place until they are puffy, about ½ hour.

Meanwhile, prepare a hot oven to 425°F, 220°C, Gas Mark 7. Bake the pastries for 7 to 10 minutes until golden brown.

Fillings

Almond Paste
Mix 1 ounce (25g) ground almonds with 1 ounce (25g) caster sugar, 1 drop of almond extract and 1 teaspoon (1 × 5ml spoon) beaten egg.

Apple and Raisin
Mix 1 dessertspoon (1 × 10ml spoon) chopped seedless raisins with 2 tablespoons (2 × 15ml spoons) grated apple, ¼ teaspoon (1 × 1.25ml spoon) grated orange rind, 1 dessertspoon (1 × 10ml spoon) demerara sugar and a pinch of mixed spice.

Cinnamon
Mix 1 ounce (25g) butter, 1 ounce (25g) caster sugar and 1 teaspoon (1 × 5ml spoon) ground cinnamon. Mix in 1 teaspoon (1 × 5ml spoon) each of currants and cut mixed peel.

Vanilla Cream
In a small saucepan mix 1 tablespoon (1 × 15ml spoon) beaten egg with 1 teaspoon (1 × 5ml spoon) flour and 1 teaspoon (1 × 5ml spoon) caster sugar. Beat in 2 fluid ounces (50ml) milk, bring to boil, stirring. Remove from the heat and add 1 teaspoon (1 × 5ml spoon) vanilla extract.

Tivoli Pastries

Eight 2 × 2in (5 × 5cm) pastries

¼ quantity Danish Pastries recipe
1 quantity Apple and Raisin filling
½ quantity Vanilla Cream filling
Egg Glaze (opposite)

Decoration
1 tablespoon (1 × 15ml spoon) thin Glacé Icing*
Flaked almonds

Roll out the dough and trim to an 8 × 4in (20 × 10cm) oblong. Cut into eight 2in (5cm) squares.

Spread a little Apple and Raisin filling diagonally across four squares. Spread the Vanilla Cream filling over four squares. Fold over two opposite corners to enclose the filling and overlap in the centre. Brush with the glaze then press lightly to seal. Place on a baking sheet and leave in a warm place until they are puffy, about ½ hour.

Prepare a hot oven at 425°F, 220°C, Gas Mark 7. Bake the pastries for 7 to 10 minutes until golden brown. Drizzle Glacé Icing over while still hot and scatter flaked almonds over.

Stars

Eight 2 × 2in (5 × 5cm) stars

¼ quantity Danish Pastries recipe
1 quantity Almond Paste filling
Egg Glaze (opposite)

Decoration
1 tablespoon (1 × 15ml spoon) thin Glacé Icing*
4 glacé cherries, chopped

Roll out the dough and trim to an 8 × 4in (20 × 10cm) oblong. Cut into eight 2in (5cm) squares and brush with Egg Glaze. Roll the filling into eight balls and place one in the centre of each square.

Cut the corner of each square diagonally ⅜in (1cm) towards the centre. Fold alternate points on to the Almond Paste, pressing firmly on top to secure. Place pastries on a baking sheet, brush with the glaze and leave in a warm place until they are puffy, about ½ hour.

Meanwhile, prepare a hot oven at 425°F, 220°C, Gas Mark 7. Bake the pastries for 7 to 10 minutes until golden brown. Drizzle Glacé Icing over while still hot and decorate with glacé cherry pieces.

Spandauers

Eight 1½ × 1½in (3.5 × 3.5cm) spandauers

¼ quantity Danish Pastries recipe
Egg Glaze (opposite)
2 canned or fresh apricot halves, chopped
½ quantity of Vanilla Cream filling

Decoration
2 tablespoons (2 × 15ml spoons) Apricot Glaze*
1 tablespoon (1 × 15ml spoon) thin Glacé Icing*
Flaked almonds

Roll out the pastry and trim to a 6 × 3in (15 × 7.5cm) oblong.

Cut into eight 1½in (3.5cm) squares. Brush over with Egg Glaze.

Divide apricots between the squares. Fold each point to meet in the centre and press gently to seal. Divide the Vanilla Cream filling between the pastries, putting a little in the centre of each. Place pastries on a baking sheet and leave in a warm place to become puffy, about ½ hour.

Meanwhile, prepare a hot oven at 425°F, 220°C, Gas Mark 7. Bake the pastries for 7 to 10 minutes until golden brown.

Brush them with Apricot Glaze after baking, then drizzle Glacé Icing over them and scatter flaked almonds over.

Pinwheels

Eight 1½ × 1½in (3.5 × 3.5cm) pinwheels

¼ quantity Danish Pastries recipe
1 quantity Cinnamon filling
Egg Glaze (opposite)

Decoration
1 tablespoon (1 × 15ml spoon) thin Glacé Icing*
Flaked almonds

Roll out the pastry and trim to an oblong 10 × 4in (25 × 10cm). Spread with filling and roll up from the short side. With a sharp knife cut into eight slices and place cut side down on a greased baking sheet. Brush the pastries with the glaze and leave in a warm place until they are puffy, about ½ hour.

Meanwhile, prepare a hot oven at 425°F, 220°C, Gas Mark 7. Bake the pastries for 7 to 10 minutes until golden brown. Drizzle Glacé Icing over and scatter flaked almonds over.

Biscuits

Crisp lacy biscuits can be served with tea or desserts. When shaped into baskets or cornets they can be filled with creams, mousses or ice cream. Buttery biscuit mixtures are shaped by piping and swirling, and soft sponge mixtures make delicious drops, pretzels and fingers.

Ground Almond Biscuits

Mix, match, flavour and shape these biscuits to make an attractive selection. The flavour improves with storage.

Ground Almond Rosettes

Eight ¾in (2cm) rosettes or ten 2in (5cm) fingers

Rice paper
2 ounces (50g) ground almonds
2 ounces (50g) icing sugar
1 egg white

Glaze
1 egg white, beaten

Decoration
8 shelled almonds
3 glacé cherries, chopped
20 shelled hazelnuts
10 angelica pieces

Cover a baking sheet with rice paper. Prepare a piping bag fitted with a star potato tube.

Place ground almonds and icing sugar in a small bowl and mix together. Add sufficient egg white to make a smooth paste. Place mixture in a piping bag and pipe mixture on to baking tray, shaping as described below. Leave overnight to dry.

Prepare a hot oven at 450°F, 230°C, Gas Mark 8. Brush biscuits with egg white to glaze.

Bake biscuits for 4 to 5 minutes until just beginning to brown at the edges. Remove from the oven and cool on a wire rack. These biscuits will keep up to three weeks in an airtight tin.

Rosettes
Pipe rosettes ¾in (2cm) in diameter. Place a shelled almond and three small pieces of glacé cherry in the centre of each one.

Fingers
Pipe 2in (5cm) fingers. Place a shelled hazelnut at each end and an angelica leaf in the centre of each.

Flavours
Lemon
Stir 2 teaspoons (2 × 5ml spoons) lemon rind into the almond mixture. Decorate with small pieces of lemon jelly sweets after baking.

Orange
Stir 2 teaspoons (2 x 5ml spoons) orange rind into the almond mixture. Decorate with pieces of orange jelly sweet after baking.

Ginger
Decorate with slices of stem ginger.

Previous pages, clockwise from left *Brandy Snap Fan and Brandy Snap (page 65); Walnut Ratafias (opposite); Duet Wreath (page 69) surrounded by Nut Tuile (page 65), Spiced Flower (page 69), Orange Finger (page 68), Duet (page 69) and Coupelle Cornet (page 65); Orange and Almond Cigar (page 66); plain and chocolate-coated Florentines (page 66); 1in (2.5cm) Sponge Drops (page 69) surrounded by Sponge Drop Oysters and Sponge Fingers and Pretzels (all page 69), Coffee Kisses (right); Ratafias (right); Coffee Sponge Drops (page 69).*

Coffee Kisses

Eight ¾in (2cm) rosettes

1 quantity Ground Almond Rosettes recipe using
  caster sugar instead of icing sugar
2 teaspoons (2 × 5ml spoons) instant coffee
Granulated sugar, to coat
2 tablespoons (2 × 15ml spoons) coffee-flavoured
  Rich Butter Cream*
1 tablespoon (15ml spoon) icing sugar, to dust
  (optional)

Prepare a moderately hot oven at 350°F, 180°C, Gas
Mark 4. Grease a baking sheet.

Make mixture as for Ground Almond Rosettes,
stirring in instant coffee and making it stiff enough
to handle. Divide mixture into 16 and lightly shape
each portion into a ball. Roll ball in remaining egg
white then in granulated sugar, to coat.

Place balls a little apart on the baking sheet and
lightly flatten. Bake 10 to 15 minutes until set and
crazed. Remove from the baking sheet and cool on a
wire rack.

To serve, sandwich biscuits together in pairs.
Dust with icing sugar, if desired.

Ratafias

Twelve to fourteen 1in (2.5cm) ratafias

1 quantity Ground Almond Rosettes recipe using
  caster sugar instead of icing sugar
Few drops almond extract
12 to 14 blanched almonds, optional

Prepare a cool oven at 275°F, 140°C, Gas Mark 1.
Grease and flour a baking sheet. Prepare a piping
bag fitted with a ½in (2.5cm) plain tube.

Place caster sugar, ground almonds and almond
extract in a small saucepan with the egg white, but
reserve 1 teaspoon (5ml spoon) egg white. Beat
ingredients thoroughly together. Place pan over a
low heat and cook 3 to 4 minutes until the mixture
thickens and comes away from the base of the pan.
Cool slightly then place mixture in a piping bag and
pipe small rounds or shape small neat heaps on the
baking sheet. Top each with an almond, if desired.
Half way through cooking, brush over with reserved
egg white; bake 15 to 20 minutes until set and lightly
coloured. Remove ratafias from the baking sheet
and cool on a wire rack.

These biscuits will keep up to three weeks in an
airtight tin.

Variation
Use ground walnuts instead of ground almonds,
shape into rough mounds and bake for 20 to 25
minutes.

Lebkuchen

These spicy, honey-flavoured biscuits are of German origin and their dark gold
colour looks good with swirls and stars of icing, or nuts and glazes. The mixture
can be shaped in many ways and will store well, either raw or cooked.

Lebkuchen

Forty 1½in (3.5cm) biscuits

1 ounce (25g) moist brown sugar
1 ounce (25g) butter
4 level dessertspoons (4 × 10ml spoons) clear honey
4 ounces (100g) plain flour
½ teaspoon (1 × 2.5ml spoon) mixed spice
Pinch of ground cinnamon
Pinch of ground ginger
Pinch of bicarbonate of soda

Place sugar and butter in a small saucepan and
carefully measure honey into it. Heat gently until

the butter has melted. Remove from heat and cool.

Sift flour, spice, cinnamon, ginger and
bicarbonate of soda together. Add to the saucepan
and beat until mixture forms a ball. Knead dough on
a lightly floured surface until smooth; wrap in cling
film and leave dough in the refrigerator for 1 hour.

Heat oven to 375°F, 190°C, Gas Mark 5. Grease
two baking sheets and prepare decorations as in the
following recipes. Roll out dough to ¼in (6mm)
thickness, cut out shapes and bake for 8 to 10
minutes until biscuits are pale golden in colour. Lift
off baking sheet and cool on a wire rack. Decorate
as described below. Store in an airtight tin.

Lebkuchen Hearts

Ten 1½in (4cm) biscuits

¼ quantity Lebkuchen dough, as recipe
   (page 61)
2 tablespoons (2 × 15ml spoons) pink Quick
   Fondant Icing*
10 crystallized violets

Cut out and cook 1½in (4cm) heart-shaped
Lebkuchen and cool on a wire rack. Decorate each
heart with pink icing and place a crystallized violet
on each one.

Pecan Praline

Twenty-five 1in (2.5cm) biscuits

½ quantity Lebkuchen dough, as recipe
   (page 61)
2 ounces (50g) sugar
25 pecan nuts

Cut out and cook 1in (2.5cm) round Lebkuchen.
Cool on a wire tray.
   Place sugar in a small heavy-based saucepan and
place over a moderate heat until sugar begins to
melt. Add shelled pecan nuts and stir caramel until
nuts are evenly coated with syrup. Using a teaspoon
(5ml spoon), place one pecan nut with a little syrup
on each biscuit. Work quickly before the caramel
becomes brittle.
   The remaining mixture can be turned on to an
oiled baking sheet and crushed to use as
decorations for desserts.

Meringue-Topped Lebkuchen

Forty ¾in (2cm) biscuits

Icing sugar, as required
½ egg white, beaten
1 quantity Lebkuchen dough, as recipe
   (page 61)
5 glacé cherries, chopped

Stir sufficient icing sugar into half a beaten egg
white to form a stiff consistency. Cut out the biscuits
and place on a baking sheet. Place a small blob of
meringue in the centre of each. Bake for 1 or 2
minutes longer than the basic Lebkuchen recipe.
Decorate each with a piece of glacé cherry
immediately. Cool on a wire tray.

Sesame Lebkuchen

Twenty 1½in (3.5cm) biscuits

½ quantity Lebkuchen dough, as recipe
   (page 61)
3 tablespoons (3 × 15ml spoons) sesame seeds

Sprinkle a lightly floured surface with sesame seeds
and roll out the dough on top. Cut out shapes as
desired, invert on to baking sheet.

Harlequin Aces

Twenty-five ¾in (2cm) biscuits

½ quantity Lebkuchen dough, as recipe
   (page 61)
1 egg yolk
4 shades food colouring

Using petits fours cutters, cut out tiny Lebkuchen
and place them on the baking sheet. Beat 1 egg yolk
with a few drops of water and divide the yolk
between four egg cups. Colour each one with food
colouring and brush the yolk over the kuchen. Bake
3 to 4 minutes – do not overcook.

Royal Stars

Ten 1½in (4cm) biscuits

¼ quantity Lebkuchen dough, as recipe
   (page 61)
½ egg yolk
30 pine nuts

Using a star cutter, cut out Lebkuchen and place
them on a baking sheet. Mix half an egg yolk with 3
drops of water and use to glaze the kuchen. Arrange
3 pine nuts on each and bake as recipe.

To hang biscuits
Make a small hole in the biscuits before
baking, so that the baked biscuits can be
threaded with ribbon.

Right Selection of Ground Almond Rosettes and
2in (5cm) Fingers (page 60).

Langues des Chats

These buttery biscuits can be shaped into fingers, circles and curls. They store well and are useful to serve with ice creams and softly set desserts.

Langues des Chats

Forty 2½in (6cm) langues des chats

1 ounce (25g) butter, softened
1 ounce (25g) caster sugar
Few drops vanilla extract
½ beaten egg (small)
1 ounce (25g) plain flour

Prepare a moderately hot oven at 400°F, 200°C, Gas Mark 6. Grease two baking sheets. Prepare a large Piping Bag* from non-stick baking parchment.

Place butter, sugar and vanilla extract in a bowl and beat until light and fluffy. Beat in the egg, then fold in the flour. Place the mixture in the piping bag and snip off the end to make a ⅜in (1cm) hole. Pipe mixture in 2½in (6cm) lengths on to the prepared baking sheets, leaving room between each one for spreading. Bake 3 to 4 minutes until light golden on the edges.

Remove tray from the oven and quickly and gently lift biscuits with a palette knife. Leave to cool on a rack. When cold, store in an airtight tin.

Coconut and Cheese Snaps

Twenty-four 1½in (4cm) snaps

1 quantity Langues des Chats recipe, omitting vanilla extract and using 2 ounces (50g) full fat cream cheese instead of butter
1 tablespoon (1 × 15ml spoon) desiccated coconut
1 ounce (25g) caster sugar
2 tablespoons (2 × 15ml spoons) dried coconut slices

Heat oven and prepare baking sheets as for Langues des Chats recipe. Grease a small rolling pin or thick wooden handles for shaping. Make up the mixture using the cheese instead of the butter. Stir in the desiccated coconut and extra caster sugar.

Using a teaspoon (5ml spoon), drop six half spoonfuls of mixture well apart on the baking sheets. Spread mixture out to 1¼in (3cm). Sprinkle generously with coconut flakes on each one. Bake 4 to 5 minutes until the biscuits are just beginning to brown round the edges. Quickly remove from the baking sheets and leave to set over the rolling pin or handles. When cold, store in an airtight tin.

Sesame Sticks

Forty 2½in (6cm) sticks

1 quantity Langues des Chats recipe
2 teaspoons (2 × 5ml spoons) sesame seeds

Follow the Langues des Chats recipe, but stir the sesame seeds into the mixture before filling the piping bag.

Walnut Viscontes

Twenty 1in (2.5cm) biscuits

2 glacé cherries
1 ounce (25g) ground walnuts
½ quantity Langues des Chats mixture

Prepare the oven and baking sheets as in the Langues des Chats recipe.

Finely chop the cherries and mix with the ground walnuts. Stir into the mixture.

Using a teaspoon (5ml spoon), drop six half spoonfuls of mixture on to a baking sheet and spread each out to 1in (2.5cm). Bake until just beginning to brown on the edges. Quickly remove from the sheet and cool the biscuits on a wire tray.

Repeat with remaining mixture.

To avoid breaking the biscuits
Do not cover the baking sheet with too many biscuits as they quickly become brittle once removed from the oven.

Coupelles

Perfect for baskets, cornets and tiny rolls, this mixture can be flavoured and attractively shaped. Store the biscuits between non-stick parchment.

Coupelles

Twenty 1½in (4cm) biscuits and eight 3in (7.5cm) baskets or cornets, or eighteen 3in (7.5cm) cigars

2 ounces (50g) butter
2 egg whites
2½ ounces (65g) caster sugar
2 ounces (50g) plain flour, sifted
Oil for brushing

Prepare a moderate oven at 375°F, 190°C, Gas Mark 5. Line two or three baking sheets with non-stick baking parchment. Brush with oil.

Melt butter gently in a small saucepan and remove from heat. Place egg whites in a medium bowl and beat for 1 minute until frothy. Add sugar and beat a further 2 to 3 minutes until thick. Fold in the flour with the butter.

Using a teaspoon (5ml spoon) drop three half spoonfuls of the mixture well apart on the prepared trays. Spread each to about a 1½in (4cm) circle with the back of the spoon. Bake 3 to 4 minutes until just turning golden brown at the edges.

Working quickly, remove the biscuits with a palette knife and shape (see below). Leave to cool on a wire tray. When cold, store in an airtight tin.

Ease each biscuit off the tray first, then leave there while shaping the others. This prevents sticking.

Curves
Grease the handle of a large wooden spoon and lay the hot biscuits over it until set.

Cornets
Follow recipe for Coupelle Baskets (page 66) but wrap biscuits round greased cream horn tins.

Cigars
Wrap biscuits tightly round greased wooden spoon handles and hold a few minutes until set.

Shaping biscuits
Always spread the mixture out on cooled trays and use a light, circular movement. Never attempt to cook more than 3 biscuits at once.

Nut Tuiles

Fourteen 2½in (6cm) tuiles or thirty 1in (2.5cm) biscuits

1 ounce (25g) hazelnuts, finely chopped
½ uncooked Coupelles mixture, as recipe

Prepare oven and baking sheet as described in Coupelles recipe. Grease a wooden spoon handle for shaping. Stir the nuts into the mixture. Using a teaspoon (5ml spoon) place 3 spoonfuls – half spoonfuls (2.5ml spoons) for smaller biscuits – well apart on the baking sheet. Spread mixture to about 2½in (6cm) – or 1½ (4cm) – circle. Bake.

When just beginning to brown at the edges, remove from baking sheet and leave to set over a wooden spoon handle. When cold, store in an airtight tin. Wipe parchment and repeat with remaining mixture.

Brandy Snaps

Ten 2½in (6cm) snaps or fans

½ quantity Coupelles recipe, omitting egg white
1 ounce (25g) golden syrup
½ teaspoon (1 × 2.5ml spoon) ground ginger

Prepare oven and line three baking sheets with non-stick baking parchment. Grease three wooden spoon handles.

Melt syrup gently with the butter and sugar in a small pan, or microwave oven. Stir in flour and ginger. Using a teaspoon (5ml spoon), place 3 level spoonfuls of mixture well apart on the parchment and spread out. Bake 7 to 10 minutes. When light golden in colour, remove from the oven, wait 30 seconds then quickly remove from the tray and roll quickly round the handles. When set, slide off and leave to cool on a wire rack. Wipe parchment and repeat with remaining mixture.

Fans
To shape, fold the biscuit quickly into four and lift up the edges to make a frill.

Coupelle Baskets

Eight 3in (7.5cm) baskets

½ uncooked Coupelles mixture, as recipe (page 65)
Large pinch ground cinnamon

Prepare oven and baking sheets as in the basic recipe. Grease two or three brioche tins, deep patty tins or small oranges, for shaping.

Follow basic recipe, folding in cinnamon sifted with the flour.

Using a rounded teaspoon (5ml spoon), place mounds of mixture well apart on baking sheets and spread each out to a 3in (7.5cm) circle. Bake. When just beginning to brown at the edges, remove biscuits from the tray and quickly mould each inside a tin or over an orange, shaping with the fingers. Leave for 1 minute to set, then place basket on a cooling rack.

Wipe parchment and repeat with remaining mixture.

Orange and Almond Cigars

Eighteen 3in (7.5cm) cigars

1 tablespoon (1 × 15ml spoon) ground almonds
2 teaspoons (2 × 5ml spoons) grated orange rind
½ uncooked Coupelles mixture, as recipe (page 65)
2 ounces (50g) dessert chocolate
½ teaspoon (2.5ml) kirsch

Heat oven and prepare baking sheets as described in the Coupelles recipe. Grease small wooden handles for shaping.

Stir almonds and orange rind into the mixture. Using a teaspoon (5ml spoon), drop 3 level spoonfuls of mixture on to a baking sheet and spread each to an oval. Bake 4 to 5 minutes until lightly browned at the edges.

Remove biscuits from the tray and wrap immediately round the prepared handles. Leave to set, then slide them off the handles and cool the cigars on a wire tray. Repeat with remaining mixture.

Melt chocolate and kirsch in a small basin over hot water and dip one end of each cigar in this mixture to coat. Leave to dry.

Florentines

Twenty 2½in (6cm) florentines

Use ½ quantity Coupelles recipe (page 65), omitting
*   egg white and half the flour*
1 ounce (25g) flaked almonds
1 ounce (25g) glacé cherries
1 ounce (25g) candied peel
2 tablespoons (2 × 15ml spoons) whipped cream
Rice paper or non-stick baking parchment

To coat
6 ounces (150g) dessert chocolate

Heat oven to 350°F, 180°C, Gas Mark 4. Line two baking sheets with rice paper or baking parchment.

Roughly crush the almonds. Finely chop the cherries and candied peel. Melt butter and sugar together gently in a small saucepan or microwave oven. Stir in the flour, almonds, cherries and peel. Fold in the cream.

Using a teaspoon (5ml spoon), place 3 level spoonfuls of mixture well apart on prepared trays. Lightly flatten. Bake 8 to 10 minutes until edges are light golden in colour. Remove tray from oven. Remove rice paper complete with the Florentines and leave to cool on the paper. When cold cut neatly round each one with scissors. If using baking parchment, wait 30 seconds after removing the tray from the oven, then quickly remove the Florentines and leave them to cool on a wire rack. Repeat with the remaining mixture.

To coat with chocolate, break up the chocolate and melt in a small basin over hot water, or in a microwave oven. Using a small palette knife, spread the chocolate on the underside of each Florentine and leave to dry, chocolate side uppermost. When dry, store Florentines in an airtight tin.

Traditional Florentines
Traditionally the chocolate is patterned with a fork. If serving Florentines without the chocolate coating, then cook them on non-stick baking parchment to capture a delicate lacy effect.

Right, clockwise from top left *2½in (6cm) Brandy Snaps (page 65); Coupelle Baskets (above); Coupelles (page 65); Brandy Snap Fans (page 65).*

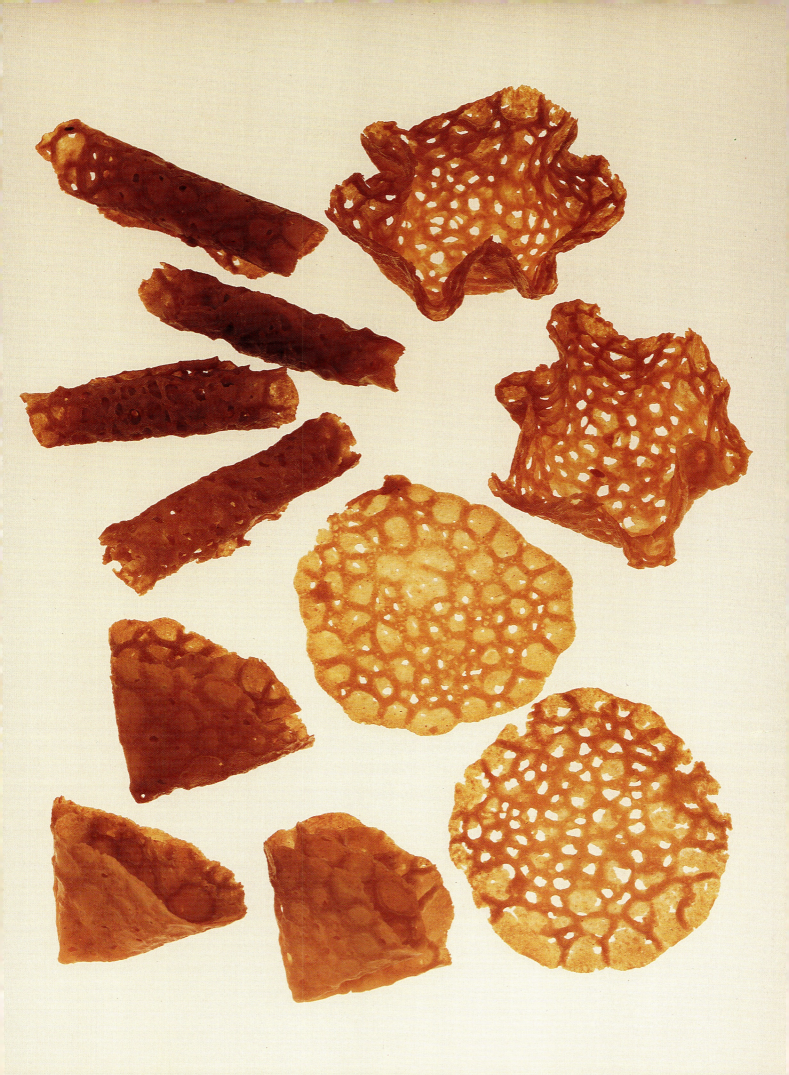

Piped Biscuits

This mixture is excellent for piping delicate biscuits. It holds its shape well and may be used with a biscuit cutter or moulded on to a biscuit tray. A recipe for sponge fingers – also piped but made with egg rather than butter – is included in this section.

Piped Biscuits

Sixteen 2½in (6cm) fingers or twenty-four smaller biscuits

2 ounces (50g) butter, softened
2 dessertspoons (2 × 10ml spoons) icing sugar
Few drops vanilla extract
2 ounces (50g) plain flour

Prepare a moderate oven at 350°F, 180°C, Gas Mark 4. Grease 2 baking sheets.

Place butter, sugar and vanilla extract in a bowl and beat until pale and fluffy. Stir in the flour. Place mixture in a piping bag fitted with a small star potato tube and pipe shapes on to the baking sheets, as described in the following recipes. Bake 10 to 15 minutes until just beginning to turn pale golden in colour.

Remove from the baking sheets and cool on a wire rack. When cold, store in an airtight tin.

Freezing
The Piped Biscuits mixture may be rolled into two 1in (2.5cm) wide sausage shapes and frozen. To use, part thaw then cut into thin slices and bake as instructed.
Alternatively, thaw completely and shape or pipe as required.

Orange Fingers

Eight 2½in (6cm) fingers

2 teaspoons (2 × 5ml spoons) grated orange rind
½ quantity Piped Biscuits mixture, as recipe

Stir orange rind into the mixture. Pipe 2½in (6cm) long fingers on to a greased baking sheet. Bake as directed in the Piped Biscuits recipe and then cool on a wire rack.

Lemon Oysters

Twenty 1in (2.5cm) shells; 10 oysters

Grated rind of half a lemon
½ quantity Piped Biscuits mixture, as recipe
2 tablespoons (2 × 15ml spoons) Chocolate Fudge Icing*
Icing sugar to dust

Stir lemon rind into the mixture. Use a large star potato tube and pipe shells about ¾in (2cm) wide on a greased baking sheet. Bake, then cool on a wire rack.

Sandwich two shells together at the base with Chocolate Fudge Icing to make an oyster. Dust with icing sugar.

Ingredients, sauces, edible containers, etc that are asterisked in the recipes on these pages are given in detail on pages 147 to 156. For exact page numbers, refer to the index at the end of the book.

Spiced Flowers

Eight 1in (2.5cm) flowers

Large pinch mixed spice
½ quantity Piped Biscuits mixture, as recipe
1 glacé cherry
Icing sugar to dust

Stir spice into the mixture. Pipe stars of mixture about 1in (2.5cm) wide on a greased baking sheet. Cut the cherry into eight small pieces and place one in the centre of each. Bake as directed in the Piped Biscuits recipe, then cool on a wire rack. Dust each lightly with icing sugar.

Duets

Ten 2½in (6cm) sticks plus ten 1in (2.5cm) wreaths

1 quantity Piped Biscuits mixture as recipe, but
  replacing 1 ounce (25g) flour with the same
  weight in cornflour
2 teaspoons (2 × 5ml spoons) cocoa powder
Few drops milk

Heat oven and prepare baking sheets as in the Piped Biscuits recipe. Prepare two large Piping Bags* from non-stick baking parchment.

Place half the mixture in one bag. Stir cocoa powder and one or two drops of milk into the remaining mixture to make it the same consistency as the other half. Place chocolate mixture into the second piping bag. Snip off ends to make a ⅜in (1cm) hole.

Sticks
Pipe two 2½in (6cm) fingers side by side of one mixture and pipe one finger of the second mixture on top.

Wreaths
Draw 1in (2.5cm) circles on a piece of non-stick baking parchment. Lightly grease and place on baking sheet. Pipe eight beads, alternating colour, round inner edge of the circles. Ensure that each bead just touches the next one.

Bake biscuits 4 to 5 minutes, without colouring the plain mixture. Cool on a wire rack.

Sponge Fingers

Twelve 2½in (6cm) fingers plus ten 1in (2.5cm) sponge drops or eight 1½in (4cm) pretzels

1 ounce (25g) caster sugar
1 egg
Few drops vanilla extract
1 ounce (25g) plain flour
Sifted icing sugar for dusting

Prepare a moderate oven at 375°F, 190°C, Gas Mark 5. Grease and flour a baking sheet. Prepare two Piping Bags* from non-stick baking parchment.

Put sugar, egg and vanilla extract in a small bowl placed over hot water. Whisk until the mixture is thick and leaves a trail on the surface. Sift flour over the surface and carefully fold in.

Divide mixture between the prepared bags and cut off ends to make a ½in (1½cm) hole. Pipe 2½in (6cm) long fingers on the prepared baking sheet leaving room for spreading. Dust with icing sugar. Bake 6 to 7 minutes until pale golden. Cool on a wire rack.

Drops
Pipe the mixture into 1in (2.5cm) discs and bake as for fingers. When cold, these may be served on their own or sandwiched together, or positioned oyster fashion with icing.

Pretzels
Pipe mixture in pretzel shapes using a ⅜in (1cm) hole in the piping bag.

Flavours

Coffee
Add 1 teaspoon (1 × 5ml spoon) instant coffee to the Sponge Fingers mixture before whisking.

Chocolate
Replace 2 teaspoons (2 × 5ml spoons) flour with 2 teaspoons (2 × 5ml spoons) cocoa powder and fold into the mixture.

Orange or Lemon
Add 2 teaspoons (2 × 5ml spoons) grated rind to the basic mixture.

Cakes

Nothing is more tempting than a selection of gâteaux and tiny cakes, with an abundance of cream, nuts, fruit, chocolate and other mouthwatering delicacies. By ringing the changes on a few simple recipes, you can make a variety of cakes to tempt even the most strong-willed. Cakes, including most decorated ones, freeze well and thaw quickly, although those with glacé icing can be messy when frozen.

Butter Sponge Cakes

Make well-flavoured, firmly textured cakes by first creaming butter and sugar together. Add a variety of flavourings and bake them in different shapes. If you are in a hurry, use the quick-mix method where all the ingredients are whisked together; if you prefer the flavour of butter the traditional creaming method is best. Butter sponge stores well just wrapped in foil, and will also freeze successfully. Make the basic cake the day before if you intend to cut it into shapes – it will be easier to handle.

Butter Sponge

Sixteen 1in (2.5cm) cakes in petits fours cases, or one 5in (12.5cm) square slab

2 ounces (50g) butter, softened
2 ounces (50g) caster sugar
1 medium-sized egg, beaten
2 ounces (50g) self-raising flour, sifted or 2 ounces (50g) plain flour and 1 teaspoon (1 × 5ml spoon) baking powder
Flavouring (see following recipes)

Prepare a moderate oven at 375°F, 190°C, Gas Mark 5.
Grease and line the base of a 5in (12.5cm) square baking tin with greaseproof paper. Grease the paper.

Place the butter and sugar in a small bowl and beat with a wooden spoon, or whisk with an electric mixer, until the mixture is pale and creamy. Add the egg, a little at a time, beating well between each addition. Fold in the flour with the flavouring, using a metal spoon. Place the mixture in the prepared tin, level the top and bake for 20 to 25 minutes until well risen, firm to touch and golden brown. Leave 2 minutes, then turn the cake out on to a cooling tray and remove the paper.

When the cake is cold, cut and decorate as required.

Butter Sponge crumbs
Make crumbs from any Butter Sponge that is left over from gâteaux or other desserts, and store in the freezer. These crumbs are especially useful for uncooked desserts like the ones on pages 80-81.

Previous pages, from left *Rich Chocolate Cherry Gâteau (page 76) and Coffee and Orange Swirl Cake (page 77) on plate; Chestnut and Mango Slice (page 81).*

Honey and Rum Babas

Six 2 fl oz (50ml) babas

4 tablespoons (4 × 15ml spoons) ground almonds
A few drops of almond extract
2 tablespoons (2 × 15ml spoons) milk
1 quantity Butter Sponge mixture,
  uncooked

Syrup
4 tablespoons (4 × 15ml spoons) clear honey
Rind and juice of 1/2 lemon
2 tablespoons (2 × 15ml spoons) rum
2 ounces (50g) Toasted Chopped Almonds*

Decoration
4 tablespoons (4 × 15ml spoons) whipped cream
6 maraschino cherries

Grease and flour six 2 fl oz (50ml) ring moulds.

Stir ground almonds, almond extract and milk into cake mixture. Place mixture in a piping bag fitted with a large tube and pipe mixture into the ring moulds. Place moulds on a baking sheet and bake 10 to 15 minutes until well risen and firm. Leave 1 minute then remove from the moulds by tapping firmly on the base over a large plate.

Prepare the syrup while babas are cooking. Place honey, lemon rind and juice and 4 tablespoons (4 × 15ml spoons) water in a small saucepan, bring slowly to boil, stirring occasionally, then remove from heat and stir in the rum and nuts. Spoon a little hot syrup over each baba while still hot.

Serve warm or cold with a large rosette of cream in the centre of each with a cherry on top.

To coat ring moulds with flour
Submerge each mould completely in flour, then remove and tap hard on the base to remove excess.

Saffron and Almond Bar

One 5 × 2in (12.5 × 5cm) bar; 8 portions

1/2 quantity Butter Sponge mixture, uncooked
A few strands of saffron
A few drops almond extract
A few drops green food colouring
1/4 quantity Rich Butter Cream*
6 ounces (150g) marzipan
2 ounces (50g) dark chocolate, melted
Knob of butter

Grease and line the base of one 5 × 3in (12.5 × 7.5cm) loaf tin.

Place a piece of foil-covered cardboard down the centre.

Divide the cake mixture between two basins. Moisten the saffron with 2 teaspoons (2 × 5ml spoons) boiling water and leave to infuse. Stir into one portion the almond extract and sufficient green food colouring to make a pale green mixture. Place the almond mixture in one side of the tin and tap to level the mixture.

Strain the saffron liquid into the second bowl, and mix gently until evenly coloured. Place the mixture in the other side of the tin and place the tin on a baking sheet. Bake 15 to 20 minutes or until well risen and firm. Leave 5 minutes, then turn out and leave to cool.

Cut each cake in half lengthways and sandwich back again using half the Rich Butter Cream and alternating the green and yellow pieces. Wrap the cakes in greaseproof paper or cling film and chill for 20 minutes.

Roll out the marzipan and cut into a 5 × 7in (12.5 × 18cm) piece. Spread the marzipan with the remaining icing and roll around the cake, join underneath.

Stand the cake on its end and brush melted chocolate over the marzipan, to coat. Leave to set. Cut the bar into eight slices.

Petits Fours

Sixteen 1in (2.5cm) petits fours:
4 Strawberry Cushions, 4 Floral Crowns, 4 Regals,
4 Chocolate Boxes

A few drops vanilla extract
1 quantity Butter Sponge mixture (page 72),
*   uncooked*
2 tablespoons (2 × 15ml spoons) sieved strawberry
*   jam*
½ quantity Rich Butter Cream*
6 tablespoons (6 × 15ml spoons) warmed sieved
*   apricot jam*

Stir a few drops of vanilla extract into the sponge
mixture. Bake as for the basic recipe. Stir the
strawberry jam into the Rich Butter Cream. Split the
cake in half through the thickness and sandwich
with a thin layer of butter cream.

    To make into petit fours, cut the cake into 1in
(2.5cm) squares or, using a 1in (2.5cm) plain cutter,
cut out rounds.

    Brush warmed apricot jam around the sides and
over the top of each petit fours and decorate as
preferred (see below).

To Decorate Strawberry Cushions
1 ounce (25g) Pink Marzipan*
4 rounds of Butter Sponge, coated
*   with jam*
1 ounce (25g) Toasted Chopped Hazelnuts or
*   Almonds**
1 tablespoon (1 × 15ml spoon) Rich Butter Cream*

Roll out the Pink Marzipan, cut to fit the tops of the
cakes and cover cakes. Hold the top and bottom of
the cakes and roll in chopped nuts to coat. Decorate
each with a tiny piped star of Rich Butter Cream.

To Decorate Floral Crowns
2 ounces (50g) Green Marzipan
4 rounds of Butter Sponge, coated
*   with jam*
2 tablespoons (2 × 15ml spoons) whipped cream
4 pistachio nuts, chopped

Roll the Green Marzipan thinly and cut into strips
the height of the cakes. Roll round the sides of the
cakes to cover. Pipe the tops with cream and
decorate with pistachio nuts.

To Decorate Regals
½ ounce (12.5g) marzipan
4 squares of Butter Sponge, coated
*   with jam*
4 ounces (100g) Quick Fondant Icing*
A few drops of yellow food colouring
4 crystallized violets or rose petals

Roll the marzipan into balls and place one in the
centre of each cake. Place the cakes on a rack with a
plate underneath. Keep the Quick Fondant Icing
warm over a saucepan of hot water then spoon
some over two cakes to cover. Tint the remaining
icing pale yellow with food colouring and cover two
more cakes. Leave to set. Decorate with a
crystallized violet or rose petal.

To Decorate Chocolate Boxes
4 squares of Butter Sponge, coated
*   with jam*
Twenty 1in (2.5cm) Chocolate Squares*
2 tablespoons (2 × 15ml spoons) Rich Butter
*   Cream* or whipped cream*
A few silver dragées or chocolate coffee
*   bean sweets*

Cover each side of the cakes with a square of
chocolate. Spread the top of each with Rich Butter
Cream or whipped cream to raise the height of the
cake then place a chocolate square on top. Place the
remaining butter cream in a piping bag fitted with a
small star tube and pipe tiny stars around the joins
and a small swirl on top. Decorate with silver
dragées or chocolate coffee beans.

Ingredients, sauces, edible containers, etc
that are asterisked in the recipes on these
pages are given in detail on pages 147 to
156. For exact page numbers, refer to the
index at the end of the book.

Right from top *Selection of Petits Fours (this page): Regal
with rose petal; Strawberry Cushion; Chocolate Box;
Regal with violet; Floral Crown; selection of these on a
plate.*

Rich Chocolate Cherry Gâteau

One 5in (12.5cm) gâteau; 8 portions

Sponge
1 ounce (25g) dark chocolate, melted
½ quantity Butter Sponge mixture (page 72)

Filling
14 ounces (400g) morello cherries in syrup
1 teaspoon (1 × 5ml spoon) arrowroot
2 fluid ounces (50ml) syrup from cherries
1 tablespoon (1 × 15ml spoon) kirsch
½ pint (250ml) double cream, whipped

Decoration
1 ounce (25g) dark chocolate, melted
1 ounce (25g) white chocolate, melted
*Chocolate Flakes**

Fold melted chocolate into cake mixture and spread in a greased and lined 5 in (12.5cm) round cake tin. Bake 20 to 25 minutes until firm to the touch. Leave 2 minutes then turn cake out on to a cooling tray and remove paper. Leave until cold.

Dry the cherries on kitchen paper. Blend the arrowroot with 2 teaspoons (2 × 5ml spoons) cherry syrup in a small saucepan, add remaining syrup and cook over a low heat, stirring continuously until the syrup coats the back of the spoon. Remove from the heat and leave to cool. Stir in the kirsch.

Draw two 5in (12.5cm) semi-circles on baking parchment. Divide each semi-circle into four wedges drawing in the lines beyond the curve. Spread dark chocolate into one semi-circle and repeat with the white chocolate in the other. When set but still soft, cut the chocolate into the portions with a long-bladed knife using the extended lines as a guide. Leave the chocolate to set firmly.

Split the chocolate cake into three layers and place one on a flat cake plate. Place one-third of the whipped cream in a piping bag fitted with a large star tube and pipe three circles of cream on the base. Place cherries between the rows, then position the second cake layer on top. Lightly spread the thickened syrup over the cake and leave 5 minutes. Spread half the remaining cream thickly over the cherry syrup and position the final cake layer on top. Chill the gâteau and remaining cream (including the cream left in the piping bag) for 30 minutes.

Spread the remaining cream from the bowl thickly round the sides of the gâteau and a thin layer on top. Carefully remove the chocolate wedges from the paper and position the colours alternately on top of the cake. Press Chocolate Flakes round the side of the cake. Using the remaining cream in the piping bag, pipe eight stars of cream round the top edge of the gâteau and position a cherry on each. Chill the gâteau until ready to serve.

To freeze Chocolate Cherry Gâteau
Open-freeze the decorated gâteau, then pack in a box, or fill the gâteau and place in the freezer instead of the refrigerator before the final decorations. Wrap the cake and store up to two weeks. Thaw in the refrigerator.

Glacé Fruit Bombes

Twelve 1in (2.5cm) bombes in petits fours cases

1 ounce (25g) cornflour
1 ounce (25g) self-raising flour
Pinch of cinnamon
1 quantity Butter Sponge mixture (page 72),
*   omitting the egg*
4 glacé cherries, 4 small crystallized pineapple
*   pieces, 4 crystallized ginger pieces*
Caster sugar to dust

Stir cornflour, flour and cinnamon into basic mixture and knead until smooth. Place 12 petits fours cases on a baking sheet. Divide mixture into 12, press each into a small circle and use to mould round the pieces of fruit. Place each bombe in a paper case and cut two slits across the top of each. Sprinkle with a little sugar.

Bake in a moderate oven for 8 to 10 minutes until golden. Dust each with a little extra sugar, then leave to cool.

Whisked Torte Sponge Cakes

Firm to cut, this rich whisked sponge cake is ideal for gâteaux and small, rolled or folded cakes. Take care, when folding in the flour or egg whites, that you do not displace the air already in the mixture.

Torte Sponge

One 5in (12.5cm) cake

2 eggs, separated
2 ounces (50g) caster sugar
2 ounces (50g) self-raising flour or 2 ounces (50g) plain flour and 1 teaspoon (1 × 5ml spoon) baking powder
1 tablespoon (1 × 15ml spoon) oil
4 teaspoons (4 × 5ml spoons) boiling water
Flavouring (see following recipes)

Prepare a moderately hot oven at 350°F, 180°C, Gas Mark 4.

Grease and line the base of a 5in (12.5cm) tin with greaseproof paper. Grease the paper.

Place egg yolks, caster sugar, flour, oil and boiling water in a bowl and beat with a wooden spoon until the mixture forms a smooth batter. Whisk the egg whites until they just hold their shape and fold into the batter mixture with the flavouring. Spread the mixture into the prepared tin and bake 15 to 20 minutes until firm and golden.

Leave in the tin for 2 minutes, then remove from the tin, remove the paper and leave to cool on a wire rack.

Finish cake as in the following recipes.

Coffee and Orange Swirl Cake

One 5½in (14cm) cake; 8 portions

Cake
½ quantity Torte Sponge mixture
2 teaspoons (2 × 5ml spoons) instant coffee powder

Icing
Finely grated rind and juice of ½ orange
A few drops orange food colouring
1 quantity Rich Butter Cream*
4 ounces (100g) icing sugar
½ teaspoon (1 × 2.5ml spoon) instant coffee powder

Decoration
3 tablespoons (3 × 15ml spoons) whipped cream
1 tablespoon (1 × 15ml spoon) Glazed Orange Peel Strands*

Prepare a 7in (18cm) square baking tin as in the basic recipe. Dissolve the coffee in 1 teaspoon (1 × 5ml spoon) hot water and fold into the basic Torte Sponge mixture. Spread in the tin and bake as above. Invert on to sugared greaseproof paper. Stir the orange rind, 1 tablespoon (1 × 15ml spoon) orange juice and a few drops food colouring into the Rich Butter Cream.

To assemble the cake, remove paper from the cake and trim the edges. Spread two-thirds of the butter cream thickly over the cake to the edges, then cut the cake into five 1¼in (3cm) wide strips. Roll up the first strip and place on its end. Continue wrapping strips round to give a spiral effect. Wrap a double thickness of greaseproof paper tightly round the cake and secure. Chill the cake for 1 hour (or freeze until required).

To finish the cake, place a 1½ in (4cm) deep collar of non-stick baking parchment round the cake and secure. Add a few drops of orange juice to the icing sugar and mix to a thick coating consistency. Place 1 tablespoon (1 × 15ml spoon) icing in a small basin with a drop of orange food colouring. Place orange icing in a small greaseproof paper icing bag. Dissolve the coffee in a few drops of hot water and stir sufficient into the remaining white icing to tint. Quickly spread the coffee icing over the top of the cake, to cover. Snip the end off the piping bag containing the orange icing and pipe zig-zags on the top of the cake. Leave to set.

Remove the paper collar and spread the reserved butter cream round the side of the cake. Smooth, then mark with a serrated icing scraper.

Pipe small stars of double cream round the top edge of the cake and decorate with Glazed Orange Peel Strands.

Lime Parcels

Ten 1½in (4cm) cakes

Rind and juice of 1 lime
½ quantity Torte Sponge mixture (page 77)
2 ounces (50g) full fat cream cheese
1 ounce (25g) icing sugar
2 tablespoons (2 × 15ml spoons) double cream,
  whipped

Decoration
1½ ounces (40g) pistachio nuts, finely chopped
2 ounces (50g) icing sugar
20 long pieces Glazed Lime Peel Strands*

Grease ten 1 fl oz (25ml) deep patty tins. Stir 1 teaspoon (1 × 15ml spoon) lime rind into the cake mixture and divide between the patty tins. Bake 10 to 15 minutes until well risen and golden brown. Remove from the tins and leave to cool on a wire rack.

To make the filling, place the cream cheese in a bowl and beat until smooth. Beat in the icing sugar, remaining lime rind and 1 tablespoon (1 × 15ml spoon) lime juice. Fold in the whipped cream. Split each sponge in half and sandwich together with a little filling, spreading the remainder round the sides. Roll each one in pistachio nuts to coat.

Add a few drops of lime juice or water to the icing sugar to make a stiff icing and cover the tops of the cakes. Decorate the cakes with Glazed Lime Peel Strands.

> **To freeze decorated cakes**
> Place the cake in the centre of a strip of foil and leave on the shelf in the freezer until the decoration is firm. Lift into a box, using the foil as a sling. Cover with foil and return to the freezer. Store up to two months.

Summer Fruit Wraps

Six 3in (7.5cm) wraps

Cake
Finely grated rind of ½ lemon
½ quantity Torte Sponge mixture (page 77)

Filling
1 tablespoon (1 × 15ml spoon) caster sugar
3 ounces (75g) fraises des bois or small raspberries

Prepare a hot oven at 425°F, 220°C, Gas Mark 7. Place a piece of non-stick baking parchment on two baking trays and draw three 3in (7.5cm) circles on each. Brush the parchment with oil. Stir the lemon rind into the cake mixture. Using a tablespoon (1 × 15ml spoon) place 2 well-filled spoonsful of mixture on each circle and spread out to the edges of the circles with the back of a small spoon. Bake each tray separately for 5 to 7 minutes until the discs are set but still pale in colour.

Remove the tray from the oven and immediately loosen the discs with a palette knife. Roll them up immediately into tubes pressing two opposite sides together and leave them side by side with the joins underneath until cold.

Sprinkle sugar over strawberries or raspberries and leave to marinate. Divide the fruit between the tubes, spoon a little of the sugar syrup over and serve at once.

> **Storage**
> The sponge discs for the Summer Fruit Wraps recipe will soften if stored overnight in a plastic container. Leave at room temperature for a few hours to harden before serving.

Right *Summer Fruit Wraps (this page) with strawberry filling.*

Crunchnut Torten

One 5in (12.5cm) cake; 8 portions

Cake
2 ounces (50g) Toasted Hazelnuts*, ground
2 teaspoons (2 × 5ml spoons) milk
½ quantity Torte Sponge mixture
*   (page 77)*
One 5in (12.5cm) Meringue Disc
*   (page 120)*

Filling
1 fluid ounce (25ml) brandy
½ pint (250ml) double cream, whipped

Decoration
1 ounce (25g) glacé cherries, chopped
12 tiny Macaroons (page 129)

Fold nuts and milk into the Torte Sponge mixture and place in the prepared tin as for basic recipe. Bake and cool as recipe.

Split the cake through its thickness into two layers and place the bottom layer on a flat cake plate. Whisk the brandy into the double cream and spread one-third over the cake. Place the Meringue Disc on top and spread another third of the cream over. Position the second piece of cake on top and spread with the remaining cream.

Sprinkle chopped cherries over the top surface of the cake, then place the Macaroons round the edge of the cake.

Keep in the refrigerator until ready to serve.

Chocolate and Orange Roulade

Whipped double cream may be used instead of Rich Butter Cream, if preferred, for this recipe but the cake should be eaten within a few hours of assembling.

One 6in (25cm) long cake; 6 portions

½ quantity Torte Sponge recipe (page 77)
2 ounces (50g) melted chocolate

Filling
3 tablespoons (3 × 15ml spoons) orange
*   marmalade*
2 tablespoons (2 × 15ml spoons) Grand
*   Marnier*
½ quantity Rich Butter Cream*
Icing sugar for dusting

Prepare a 6in (15cm) square tin as for the Torte Sponge recipe. Make a basic Torte recipe stirring in the melted chocolate. Spread in the tin. Bake as for the basic recipe and invert the cake on to a piece of greaseproof paper dusted with icing sugar. Remove the paper when cold and spread the cake with marmalade.

Beat the Grand Marnier into the Rich Butter Cream and spread over the marmalade. Using the greaseproof paper, roll up the cake. Position the join underneath. Dust with icing sugar before serving.

Refrigerator Cakes

These can be quickly assembled from store cupboard ingredients. Chocolate is especially versatile and helps to set a biscuit crumb mixture. Remember to allow sufficient time to chill and set the cakes before serving.

Truffles

Eight 1in (2.5cm) truffles

2 ounces (50g) dark chocolate
Knob of butter
1 tablespoon (1 × 15ml spoon) ground almonds
1 tablespoon (1 × 15ml spoon) double cream
½ teaspoon (1 × 2.5ml spoon) orange rind
Pinch of ground nutmeg
2 teaspoons (2 × 5ml spoons) rum
3 ounces (75g) Butter Sponge crumbs (page 72)
1 tablespoon (1 × 15ml spoon) coconut flakes,
*   crushed*

Place the chocolate and butter in a basin over hot water until the chocolate has melted. Remove from the heat and stir in the ground almonds, cream, orange rind, nutmeg and rum, and beat together until well mixed.

Sprinkle in sufficient cake crumbs to make a stiff consistency; chill.

Divide the mixture into eight and mould each one in the hands to make a smooth ball. Roll the truffles in coconut flakes and place each one in a petit four case.

Place in the refrigerator for 1 hour to set.

Double Choc Fudge Cups

Twelve 1in (2.5cm) cups

Icing
2 ounces (50g) dark chocolate
1 ounce (25g) butter
2 tablespoons (2 × 15ml spoons) beaten egg
2 teaspoons (2 × 5ml spoons) sherry
3 ounces (75g) icing sugar

Filling
2 tablespoons (2 × 15ml spoons) golden
   syrup
1½ ounces (40g) butter
2 tablespoons (2 × 15ml spoons) sweetened
   cocoa powder
1 ounce (25g) Toasted Chopped Hazelnuts*
1 ounce (25g) multi-coloured glacé cherries,
   chopped
1 ounce (25g) seedless raisins
2 ounces (50g) plain biscuits, roughly crushed

To Serve
12 Chocolate Cases* made with white chocolate
12 halves glacé cherries

Place dark chocolate and butter in a small basin
over hot water until the chocolate has melted. Beat
in the egg and sherry, then remove basin from heat
and gradually beat in the icing sugar. Leave to cool.

Place golden syrup, butter and sweetened cocoa
powder in a saucepan and heat gently until melted.
Stir in hazelnuts, chopped cherries, raisins and
crushed biscuits. Stir in 1 tablespoon (1 × 15ml
spoon) chocolate icing.

When cool divide the mixture between the
Chocolate Cases, piling it up to a peak. Chill ½ hour
in the refrigerator. Leave the icing in a warm place.

To finish the cases, place the icing in a piping bag
fitted with a small star tube and pipe icing round
each biscuit mound, to coat, starting at the bottom.
Top each one with a glacé cherry half.

Chestnut and Mango Slice

One 5 × 3in (12.5 × 7.5cm) cake; 8 portions

Base
1 ounce (25g) butter
2 ounces (50g) digestive biscuits, crushed

Filling
1 small mango or sliced mango from a can
8 ounces (200g) full fat cream cheese
4 tablespoons (4 × 15ml spoons) sweetened
   chestnut purée
2 ounces (50g) Butter Sponge crumbs (page 72)
1 tablespoon (1 × 15ml spoon) rum

Decoration
2 ounces (50g) Toasted Flaked Almonds*
1 dessertspoon (1 × 10ml spoon) icing sugar

Cut a strip of non-stick baking parchment 5 × 12in
(12.5 × 30cm) and use to line the long sides and
base of a loaf tin with a base measurement of 5 × 3in
(12.5 × 7.5cm). Melt the butter gently in a small
saucepan, remove from the heat and stir in the
biscuit crumbs. Spread the crumbs evenly into the
base of the prepared tin and press lightly. Chill until
set, about ½ hour.

Peel the mango, remove the stone and slice and
chop the fruit. Place the cream cheese in a bowl and
beat until smooth. Beat in the chestnut purée and
the chopped mango. Spread half the mixture over
the biscuit base. Sprinkle half the cake crumbs on
top and press down firmly. Pour the rum over.
Carefully spread the remaining filling on top.
Sprinkle the remaining cake crumbs over; press
lightly. Bring the ends of the baking parchment over
to cover the filling and leave to set in the
refrigerator overnight. Lift the gâteau from the tin
with the parchment and place on a flat serving plate.
Remove the parchment.

To decorate the gâteau, press the almonds firmly
round the sides. Sprinkle the top with icing sugar.

Traditional Desserts

Warming, light pies and tarts, rich fruity Christmas puddings steeped in brandy, sponge mixtures and fruit desserts are all included in this chapter. Most of them are especially suitable for winter meals.

Pies and Tarts

Pies and tarts come in all kinds of guises. These traditional versions vary from festive mince pies, originally made with minced beef to give a sweet and savoury combination, to sweet syrup and meringue tarts and even a baked jam roll.

Syrup Tart

One 6in (10cm) tart; 8 portions

1/2 Biscuit Crust Pastry recipe (page 46)
1 ounce (25g) fresh white breadcrumbs
6 tablespoons (6 × 15ml spoons) golden syrup
Grated rind of 1/2 lemon
Knob of butter
1 egg, beaten
3 tablespoons (3 × 15ml spoons) cream

Heat oven to 350°F, 180°C, Gas Mark 4. Oil a 6in (10cm) cake tin which is 1in (2.5cm) deep and use the pastry to line the base and side. Sprinkle the breadcrumbs over the base of the pastry.

Place syrup, lemon rind and butter in a small pan and heat gently. Remove from heat and beat in the egg and then 3 tablespoons (3 × 15ml spoons) of cream. Pour over the breadcrumbs and place the tart in the oven. Cook for 30 minutes until set and golden brown. Remove from the oven and cool slightly.

Cut into eight wedges. Serve warm or cold with the remainder of the cream.

To remove pastry from shells
Trim the pastry carefully so that it does not overlap the edges of the shells, or it will be difficult to remove.

Mince Pies

Eight 1½in (4cm) pies

Pastry
1/2 Biscuit Crust Pastry recipe (page 46)

Filling
3 tablespoons (3 × 15ml spoons) thick mincemeat
1 teaspoon (1 × 5ml spoon) lemon juice
Few drops brandy

Glaze
2 tablespoons (2 × 15ml spoons) milk
2oz (50g) caster sugar

To serve
3 tablespoons (3 × 15ml spoons) Brandy Butter* or pouring cream

Heat oven at 375°F, 190°C, Gas Mark 5. Grease eight 1 fl oz (25ml) patty tins, about 1½in (4cm) in diameter by 1in (2.5cm) deep.

Roll out the pastry thinly and cut out eight circles, using a 2½in (6cm) cutter. Line patty tins with the pastry. Re-roll remaining pastry and cut out eight tops using a 1½in (4cm) cutter.

Place the mincemeat, lemon juice and brandy in a small bowl and mix together. Divide mincemeat between the pie cases. Brush the pastry tops with water and place moistened side downwards over the mincemeat. Seal the edges. Brush tops with milk and sprinkle with sugar.

Bake pies for 15 minutes until golden brown. Remove from the tins and return to the oven for 1 to 2 minutes if necessary to brown the sides. Sprinkle with extra sugar.

Serve warm with Brandy Butter or cream.

Previous pages, clockwise from left *Lemon Meringue Pie (opposite); 1½in (4cm) Mince Pie (right); slice of Syrup Tart (above); Christmas Pudding (page 88); Pineapple Upside-Down Pudding (page 89).*

Baked Jam Roll

One 3 × 5½in (7.5 × 14cm) roll; 8 portions

Butter for greasing
1 ounce (25g) fresh white breadcrumbs
4 ounces (100g) self-raising flour
2 ounces (50g) prepared suet
1 ounce (25g) demerara sugar
2 tablespoons (2 × 15ml spoons) beaten egg
2 fluid ounces (50ml) milk
3 rounded tablespoons (6 × 15ml spoons) firmly set
  blackcurrant jam

To serve
¼ pt (125ml) pouring cream, or Custard Sauce* or
Vanilla Ice Cream (page 136)

Prepare a moderate oven 350°F, 180°C, Gas Mark 4.
Grease thoroughly with butter a ½lb (250g) bread
tin with a base about 3 × 5½in (7.5 × 14cm). Coat
the ends liberally with some of the breadcrumbs.
Butter a piece of greaseproof paper 5½ × 15 in
(14 × 38cm). Position the paper in the tin with the
centre on the base, to extend over the sides of the
tin. Coat paper with breadcrumbs.

Place flour, suet and sugar in a bowl and mix well.
Add the egg and sufficient milk to make a stiff
dough. Knead lightly on a floured surface. Roll
dough to an oblong 7 × 10in (18 × 25cm). Spread
jam over dough to within 1in (2.5cm) of the edges.
Fold sides of the dough over and lightly roll it up.
Moisten the end and place the join underneath.

Lift the roll into the prepared tin and sprinkle
with the remaining crumbs. Fold paper over to
cover and tuck ends loosely down the sides. Bake
for 1 hour until crisp and golden brown,
uncovering the top after 30 minutes.

Lift the roll out on to a board. Use a serrated knife
and cut off ends. Slice remaining roll into eight
pieces. Serve at once with cream, Vanilla Ice Cream
or Custard Sauce.

Lemon Meringue Pies

Six 3in (7.5cm) pies

½ Shortcrust Pastry recipe (page 36)

Filling
Grated rind and juice of 1 small lemon
2 tablespoons (2 × 15ml spoons) caster sugar
4 teaspoons (4 × 5ml spoons) cornflour
1 large egg yolk, beaten
Knob of butter

Meringue
1 large egg white
2 ounces (50g) caster sugar

Heat oven to 375°F, 190°C, Gas Mark 5. Grease
thoroughly the outsides of six 3in (7.5cm) canapé
shells or 2 fl oz (5ml) patty tins. Roll out the pastry
and cut out six circles, using a 3in (7.5cm) cutter.
Press each circle on to the outer side of a shell
trimming where necessary. (Alternatively, line patty
tins with pastry, prick and bake blind for 5 minutes
near the top of the oven.) Place shells, pastry side
uppermost, on to a baking sheet and bake for 10
minutes until the pastry is golden brown and set.
Leave a few minutes to cool then carefully ease from
the shells. Return shells to the oven for 1-2 minutes
to dry off.

To make the filling, place lemon peel, sugar and
¼ pint (125ml) water in a small pan over a low heat,
and stir until sugar has dissolved, then boil for
2 minutes. Remove from the heat. Blend cornflour
with a little lemon juice, then add the remaining
juice. Strain syrup through a sieve on to the
cornflour. Return the mixture to the pan and cook
for 2 minutes, stirring continuously. Beat in the egg
yolk and butter. Cook a further minute, if necessary,
until the mixture is thick. Leave to cool.

Turn oven up to 450°F, 230°C, Gas Mark 8.

To make the meringue, whisk the egg white in a
clean bowl until fairly stiff. Add half the sugar and
continue whisking until the meringue holds its
shape. Whisk in remaining sugar.

Place half the meringue in a small piping bag
fitted with an ⅛in (6mm) star tube. Divide lemon
mixture between pastry shells and pipe three rows
of meringue 'ropes' radiating out from the base of
each shell over the lemon mixture, refilling bag
with meringue as required. Place in the oven for
2 minutes until the meringue is golden brown, then
reduce oven temperature to 300°F, 150°C, Gas Mark
2 and cook for a further 5 minutes to crisp the
meringue. Serve either warm or cold.

Fruit Puddings

Old-fashioned fruit puddings are always a delicious end to any meal. Supremely simple summer pudding packs in all the tangy fruits that are at their peak in warm weather and contrasts with the heavier winter offerings in this chapter. Crumble made with apple is truly traditional.

Apple Crumble

Eight 3 fl oz (75ml) puddings

Butter for greasing

Fruit
12 ounces (300g) prepared cooking apples
3 tablespoons (3 × 15ml spoons) sugar
½ teaspoon (1 × 2.5ml spoon) ground cinnamon
4 teaspoons (4 × 5ml spoons) fresh orange juice

Topping
3 ounces (75g) self-raising flour
2 ounces (50g) butter
1½ ounces (40g) demerara sugar

To serve
¼ pint (150ml) pouring cream, Custard Sauce* or Vanilla Ice Cream (page 136)

Heat oven to 375°F, 190°C, Gas Mark 5.

Grease eight 3 fl oz (75ml) pots with butter. Finely chop the apples and place in a medium basin with the sugar, cinnamon and orange juice. Mix well together then divide the apple between the prepared pots (fruit should fill the pots by two-thirds).

To make the topping, place flour and butter into a medium bowl. Cut up the butter, then rub it into the flour until it resembles fine breadcrumbs. Stir in the sugar. Divide crumble between the pots and lightly press on to the apples.

Bake for 15 minutes until the crumble is golden brown. Serve warm or cold with cream, Custard Sauce or Vanilla Ice Cream.

> Ingredients, sauces, edible containers, etc that are asterisked in the recipes on these pages are given in detail on pages 147 to 156. For exact page numbers, refer to the index at the end of the book.

Summer Pudding

Six 4 fl oz (100ml) puddings

Butter for greasing
10 thin slices white bread
6 ounces (125g) mixed summer fruits: strawberries, blackcurrants, blackberries, raspberries
6 ounces (150g) prepared cooking apple, sliced
2 ounces (50g) sugar
3 tablespoons (5 × 15ml spoons) pouring cream

Grease six 4 fl oz (110ml) plastic moulds thoroughly with butter. Trim the crusts from the bread, cut each slice into four and use to line the moulds, pressing the bread firmly against the base and sides. Cut the remaining bread to cover the moulds. Place the prepared mixed fruits, apple, sugar and ¼ pint (125ml) water into a medium pan and simmer fruit gently until soft to make about 1 pint (500ml) purée with plenty of liquid.

Divide the fruit and liquid between the moulds. Cover the fruit with the remaining bread. Place a piece of buttered greaseproof paper on top and weigh down with stones or scale weights. Leave overnight in the refrigerator.

To serve, gently run a knife round the edge of each pudding and invert on to a small plate. Serve chilled with pouring cream.

Right *Baked Jam Roll (page 85); 5½in (14cm) long, it is served in slices.*

Family Desserts

These recipes include variations on light sponges which are combined with syrup, fruit or other sweet ingredients then baked or steamed, as well as Christmas pudding and a dessert based on rice.

Chocolate Fudge Pudding

One 4½in (12cm) cake; 6 portions

Butter for greasing
2 ounces (50g) self-raising flour
2 ounces (50g) soft margarine
1 egg
2 ounces (50g) caster sugar
2 tablespoons (2 × 15ml spoons) cocoa powder
2 tablespoons (2 × 15ml spoons) granulated sugar
¼ pint (125ml) hot water
3 tablespoons (3 × 15ml spoons) pouring cream or
*   Custard Sauce**

Heat oven to 350°F, 180°C, Gas Mark 4. Butter a 4½in (12cm) diameter charlotte tin or deep-sided cake tin.

Place flour, margarine, egg and caster sugar into a medium bowl. Add 1 tablespoon (1 × 15ml spoon) cocoa powder. Beat ingredients until light and fluffy.

Spread mixture on to the base of the prepared tin. Stir remaining cocoa powder and granulated sugar together in a small bowl and sprinkle over the top of the cake mixture. Pour the hot water over the sugar and cocoa. Bake immediately for 30 minutes until well risen and firm.

Turn pudding out on to a warmed plate and cut into six wedges.

Serve warm with cream or Custard Sauce.

Christmas Puddings

Ten 2in (5cm) puddings

2 ounces (50g) fresh white breadcrumbs
1 ounce (25g) self-raising flour
2 ounces (50g) shredded suet
3 ounces (75g) dark brown sugar
½ teaspoon (2.5ml spoon) mixed spice
1 ounce (25g) chopped mixed nuts
3 ounces (75g) raisins (stoned)
3 ounces (75g) sultanas
1 ounce (25g) dried apricots
1 ounce (25g) glacé cherries
1 ounce (25g) dates (stoned)
½ dessert apple
2 dessertspoons (2 × 10ml spoons) black treacle
1 small egg, beaten
½ teaspoon (1 × 2.5cm spoon) brandy
Grated rind and juice of 1 lemon

To serve
3½ tablespoons (3½ × 15ml spoons) Brandy
*   Butter**

Place breadcrumbs, flour, suet, sugar, spice and nuts in a small bowl and mix together. Finely chop the raisins, sultanas, apricots, cherries and dates. Stir into breadcrumb mixture. Peel and grate the apple, and add to the bowl with black molasses, egg, brandy, lemon rind and sufficient juice to make a stiff consistency. Cover bowl and leave in a cool place for several hours or overnight.

Prepare a large saucepan for steaming. Divide mixture into ten pieces and mould each one into a ball using wetted hands. Tie each pudding in a wetted piece of muslin dusted with flour. Suspend the puddings over a large pan of boiling water by placing two wooden spoons across the top of the pan with the puddings tied on to them. The puddings should hang above the water level. Cover pan with foil, reduce heat and steam the puddings 2½ hours, replacing the water if necessary. Remove from pan and leave to cool. Remove muslin and wrap puddings in clean muslin or greaseproof paper.

To serve, reheat the puddings by steaming for 20 minutes. Serve hot with Brandy Butter.

Pineapple Upside-Down Pudding

Six 2in (5cm) puddings

Glaze
4 tablespoons (4 × 15ml spoons) demerara sugar
Walnut-sized piece of butter, melted

Decoration
5 thin slices of pineapple, cored and skinned
1 glacé cherry

Sponge
1 ounce (25g) self-raising flour
Pinch of baking powder
Pinch of ground cinnamon
1 ounce (25g) butter, softened
1 ounce (25g) caster sugar
2 tablespoons (2 × 15ml spoons) beaten egg

To serve
3 tablespoons (3 × 15ml spoons) cream or Vanilla
  Ice Cream (page 136)

Heat oven to 350°F, 180°C, Gas Mark 4. Butter thoroughly six 2 fl oz (50ml) patty tins.

Stir demerara sugar into the melted butter and divide mixture between the prepared tins. Cut each pineapple slice into four wedges and arrange three pieces on top of the sugar in each tin. Cut the cherry into 6 pieces and place one piece in the centre of the pineapple pattern.

Place flour, baking powder, cinnamon, butter, sugar and egg in a small bowl and beat well until light and creamy. Divide mixture between the tins. Bake for about 15 minutes until well risen, golden brown and firm to the touch. Place a large plate over the tins and invert the puddings on to the plate. Serve warm with cream or Vanilla Ice Cream.

Cups for steaming
As an alternative to saké cups, small individual puddings can be steamed in egg cups or dariole moulds; these will only be half full when the pudding is cooked.

Syrup Puddings

Six 2½ fl oz (60ml) puddings

Butter for greasing
6 teaspoons (6 × 5ml spoons) golden syrup
1 ounce (25g) self-raising flour
1 ounce (25g) butter, softened
1 ounce (25g) caster sugar
Pinch of baking powder
2 tablespoons (2 × 15ml spoons) beaten egg

To serve
Golden syrup

Prepare a large steamer. Grease six 2½ fl oz (60ml) saké cups with butter.

Place 1 teaspoon (1 × 5ml spoon) syrup into the base of each cup. Place flour, butter, sugar, baking powder and egg into a bowl. Beat ingredients until light and fluffy. Divide mixture between prepared cups. Cover each cup with foil and steam for 10 minutes. Turn puddings out on to a warmed serving plate. Serve hot with golden syrup.

Creamy Rice Brûlée

Six 3 fl oz (75ml) portions

¾ pint (375ml) milk
1½ ounces (35g) short-grain pudding rice
1 ounce (25g) butter
Grated rind of 1 small orange
½ teaspoon (1.5ml spoon) nutmeg
1½ ounces (40g) sugar
1 egg yolk, beaten
3 tablespoons (3 × 15ml spoons) cream

Topping
6 dessertspoons (6 ×x 10ml spoons) demerara
  sugar

Place the milk with the rice, butter, orange rind and nutmeg in a medium pan and heat until the milk is boiling. Reduce the heat, partly cover the pan with a lid and simmer gently, stirring occasionally, for 30 minutes until the rice is soft and the mixture is creamy. Beat in the sugar and egg yolk. Stir over a low heat, if necessary, until the mixture is thick again. Remove from the heat and stir in the cream.

Prepare a moderate grill.

Divide the rice pudding between six 3 fl oz (75ml) heat-resistant pots. Sprinkle 1 dessertspoon (1 × 10ml spoon) demerara sugar over the top of each, and place under a medium-hot grill until the sugar melts and bubbles. Remove from heat. The sugar will harden on top. Serve warm.

Fruit Desserts

Fruits must be the world's first convenience foods. Attractively packaged in skins, pods or peels, they combine exotic flavours and textures with delightful colours. Marinate them in juices or fruit-based liqueurs for refreshing fruit salads or combine different kinds of berries in kissels. Firmer fruits can be cooked in compotes or flambéed in caramel syrup.

Fruit Salads

Mix fruits with complementary textures, shapes and colours to make attractive arrangements. Marinate in a syrup with a hint of liqueur, or in fruit juice, and allow the flavours to blend.

Citrus Fruit Salad

4 portions

1 grapefruit
1 large orange
2 tablespoons (2 × 15ml spoons) white rum
2 tablespoons (2 × 15ml spoons) caster sugar
4 fluid ounces (100ml) double cream
2 fluid ounces (50ml) natural low-fat yoghurt
1 small lemon
1 lime
1 teaspoon (1 × 5ml spoon) icing sugar

Cut the skin off the grapefruit and the orange then cut between the pith to remove the segments. Spread them on a plate and sprinkle with white rum and sugar. Cover and chill until ready to serve.

Whisk the cream until thick, then whisk in the yoghurt and icing sugar. Cut four thin slices from the centre of the lemon and the lime and reserve for decoration. Grate the rinds from the ends and squeeze the juice, then whisk into the cream mixture; chill.

To serve, arrange three segments of grapefruit and two of orange in a curve on four small plates and spoon the syrup over. Pipe a swirl of cream in the centre of each. Take a slice of lemon and a slice of lime together and cut each to the centre. Twist and place on the cream mixture.

Previous pages, clockwise from left *Apricots in Gewürztraminer (page 95); Frosted Fruits (page 97); Kumquat Baskets with Cream Cheese Filling (page 99); Plum with Spiced Nut Filling surrounded by Lychees with Orange Macaroon Filling (page 98); Fondant Dates (page 97); Prunes in Port (page 96); Chocolate-Coated Strawberry and Cape Gooseberry (page 97); Fondant Cape Gooseberry (page 97); Red Fruit Kissel (page 100).*

Mediterranean Date Salad

For each portion

1 fresh date
1 piece peeled mango
4 balls Ogen melon
3 slices fresh fig
1 tablespoon (1 × 15ml spoon) lemon juice
1 teaspoon (1 × 5ml spoon) Cointreau

Remove the stone from the date and press the mango in the cavity. Arrange on a serving plate with the melon and fig. Sprinkle with lemon juice mixed with Cointreau.

Melon Salad

4 portions

1 wedge water melon
1 small wedge honeydew melon
1 piece stem ginger
Juice of 1 lime
1 tablespoon (1 × 15ml spoon) syrup from ginger jar

Remove the seeds from the melons and cut the fruit in balls. Arrange on four plates a ring of water melon with a ring inside of honeydew melon. Chop the stem ginger and place in the centre.

Mix the lime juice and ginger syrup and pour over the melon. Chill until ready to serve.

Irish Strawberry Rings

4 portions

2 ounces (50g) raspberries plus 4 whole raspberries
1 ounce (25g) caster sugar
2 fluid ounces (50ml) double cream
2 fluid ounces (50ml) Bailey's cream liqueur
10 strawberries, sliced
4 slices fresh lime

Place 2 ounces (50g) raspberries in a small saucepan and heat until the juice runs. Add the caster sugar and bring to boil. Sieve into a basin, cool then chill.

Whip the cream until thick, whip in the liqueur and most of the raspberry purée, reserving 2 tablespoons (2 × 15ml spoons) in the bowl.

Place a slice of lime in the centre of each plate and arrange the sliced strawberries around. Spoon a little raspberry purée on each ring and place a raspberry in the centre of each lime slice. Serve with the cream mixture.

Green Fruit Salad

3 portions

1 lime
6 tablespoons (6 × 15ml spoons) Sugar Syrup*
1 teaspoon (1 × 5ml spoon) Kümmel
½ a ripe avocado
¼ of a green-skinned apple
1 kiwi fruit
9 honeydew melon balls
6 grapes, halved
3 fluid ounces (75ml) fromage frais

Grate the rind from the ends of the lime. Cut three thin slices from the centre and reserve for garnish. Squeeze the juice and add to the syrup with the Kümmel. Peel and slice the avocado and place in the syrup. Slice the apple, cut in wedges, and place in the syrup.

Arrange the fruit on three small plates with slices of avocado on one side, wedges of apple alongside, kiwi slices, melon balls and grapes. Cut each slice of lime to the centre, twist and place on the fruit.

Spoon a little fruit syrup over each portion and serve at once with fromage frais.

Tropical Fruit Salad

4 portions

6 tablespoons (6 × 15ml spoons) Sugar Syrup*
1 passion fruit
1 nectarine, cut in 12 slices
1 star fruit, cut in 4 slices
12 wedges fresh pineapple
3 kiwi fruit, cut in 12 slices

Boil the sugar syrup with the scooped-out seeds of the passion fruit for 2 minutes then sieve into a basin. Add the nectarine, star fruit, pineapple and kiwi fruit. Cover and chill for 2 hours.

Arrange on each of four plates three slices nectarine overlapping, one star fruit slice at the end, then three slices pineapple and three slices kiwi fruit. Pour the syrup over and serve chilled.

Orange Fruit Medley

For each portion

6 tablespoons (6 × 15ml spoons) Sugar Syrup*
1 tablespoon (1 × 15ml spoon) lemon juice
3 slices peeled tamarillo
3 slices kumquat
3 slices paw-paw, seeds removed
2 grapes
1 teaspoon (1 × 5ml spoon) white rum

Place Sugar Syrup and lemon juice in a small saucepan and add the slices of tamarillo, kumquat and paw-paw. Bring to boil, remove from the heat and leave to cool. Arrange the fruit on a plate, with the paw-paw in a curve and the tamarillo and kumquat alternately overlapping. Cut the grapes in slices and arrange in a fan shape.

Boil the syrup to reduce it by half. Add the white rum and trickle over the fruit.

Fruit Compotes

The fruits in a compote can be fresh or dried, and of a single variety or mixed to blend flavours and textures. Include lime or lemon juice or dry white wine to balance the sweetness of the syrup and add a strongly flavoured liqueur. Compotes improve if chilled overnight to allow the flavours to blend.

Spiced Apple Compote

6 portions

¼ pint (125ml) cider
1 cinnamon stick
2 cloves
1 vanilla pod
2 tablespoons (2 × 15ml spoons) Apricot Glaze*
2 ounces (50g) light moist brown sugar
Shredded rind of half an orange
1 pound (500g) small cooking apples
Juice of half an orange
1 ounce (25g) Toasted Flaked Almonds*

Boil cider with the cinnamon stick and cloves for 5 minutes. Remove from the heat, add the vanilla pod and leave until cold; strain. The vanilla pod can be dried and re-used. Place the Apricot Glaze, sugar and the spiced stock in a large shallow saucepan and heat to dissolve the sugar. Add the orange rind and cook for 5 minutes.

Peel the apples, cut in quarters and remove the core. Cut into ½in (1.25cm)-thick slices and spread in the boiling syrup in a single layer. Return to boil and cook very slowly until tender but still firm. Remove from the heat and add the orange juice. Cover and leave until cold.

Serve in small bowls with a sprinkling of Toasted Flaked Almonds.

Left, from top *Melon Salad (page 92); Orange Fruit Medley (page 93); Mediterranean Date Salad (page 92); Tropical Fruit Salad (page 93); Irish Strawberry Ring (page 93).*

Apricots in Gewürztraminer

6 portions

4 ounces (100g) whole dried apricots
½ pint (250ml) Gewürztraminer wine
1 strip orange rind
1 tablespoon (1 × 15ml spoon) clear honey
2 ounces (50g) green grapes
Soured cream, optional

Place the apricots and wine in a glass or stainless-steel saucepan and bring to boil. Remove from the heat and leave overnight.

The next day, add the orange rind and honey and bring to boil. Cover and simmer until the apricots are tender, about 10 minutes. Peel the grapes and remove the pips, keeping them whole. Add to the apricots and leave to cool.

Remove the orange rind. Serve with soured cream if desired.

Pears with Gin and Lime Juice

6 portions

2 limes
1 ounce (25g) caster sugar
2 small ripe pears
3 tablespoons (3 × 15ml spoons) dry gin
6 Brandy Snaps (page 65)

Remove the zest of the limes in strips. Place in a saucepan with 6 tablespoons (6 × 15ml spoons) water and simmer until tender, about 10 minutes. Add the juice of the limes and the sugar and stir until dissolved.

Peel, slice and core the pears. Place in the saucepan in a single layer and baste with juice. Cook until just tender, remove from the heat and add the gin. Leave to cool, basting occasionally with the juice.

Serve with Brandy Snaps.

Damson Compote with Armagnac

4 portions

½ pint (250ml) red wine
1 stick cinnamon
1 teaspoon (1 × 5ml spoon) grated fresh ginger
1 strip lemon rind
2 tablespoons (2 × 15ml spoons) sugar
4 ounces (100g) damsons
2 tablespoons (2 × 15ml spoons) Armagnac
¼ pint (125ml) double cream
2 tablespoons (2 × 15ml spoons) honey

Heat the wine, cinnamon, ginger and lemon rind and sugar, add the damsons and cook very slowly until the skins just break. Remove from the heat, cover and cool. Lift out the damsons with a draining spoon and place in a serving bowl.

Boil the syrup until reduced by half, add the Armagnac and strain over the damsons. Cool, then chill.

Serve with whipped double cream sweetened with honey.

Prunes in Port

6 portions

¼ pint (125ml) water
1 strip orange rind
1 ounce (25g) sugar
¼ pint (125ml) ruby port
4 ounces (100g) large pitted prunes
1 ounce (25g) marzipan
12 blanched almonds
3 fluid ounces (75ml) soured cream

Place the water, orange rind and sugar in a saucepan, cover and simmer for 5 minutes. Remove from the heat and add the port and prunes. Leave to soak overnight, then cook gently for 5 minutes. Remove the prunes with a draining spoon and boil the syrup until reduced by half. Remove the orange rind; shred finely.

Divide the marzipan into 12 pieces and press around the almonds. Press an almond into the centre of each prune and return to the syrup; sprinkle with the orange shreds.

Served chilled with soured cream.

Cherries in Red Wine

4 portions

¼ pint (125ml) water
¼ pint (125ml) red wine
1 ounce (25g) sugar
2 tablespoons (2 × 15ml spoons) redcurrant jelly
Pinch of ground cinnamon
½ pound (250g) sour cherries
1 tablespoon (1 × 15ml spoon) cherry brandy
4 small scoops Vanilla Ice Cream (page 136)

Place the water, wine, sugar and jelly in a saucepan. Bring to boil, add the cinnamon and simmer 5 minutes. Add the cherries and simmer for 10 minutes. Remove from the syrup with a draining spoon and reduce the syrup by half. Add cherry brandy and re-heat.

Serve hot with ice cream.

Ingredients, sauces, edible containers, etc that are asterisked in the recipes on these pages are given in detail on pages 147 to 156. For exact page numbers, refer to the index at the end of the book.

Dipped Fruits

A selection of bite-sized fruits with crisp sweet coatings provides the perfect finish to a meal. Choose firm whole fruits with dry skins such as grapes, cherries, strawberries and Cape gooseberries. Juice will melt the coating. Cut fruits are best coated with chocolate.

Fondant Fruits

To coat 4 ounces (100g) assorted fruits

4 ounces (100g) Quick Fondant Icing*, set
4 teaspoons (4 × 5ml spoons) Sugar Syrup*
4 ounces (100g) black and green grapes (or
  cherries, strawberries, Cape gooseberries,
  greengages, peeled lychees or fresh dates)
Food colouring (optional)

Chop the fondant and place with the syrup in a small deep basin or cup in a saucepan of boiling water. Stir occasionally until the fondant has melted.

Have ready a tray covered with non-stick baking parchment or foil. Hold the fruit by the stalk and dip into the fondant, taking care to make a neat line at the top. Remove from the icing, invert and turn gently until the fondant has set. Place on the lined tray and leave at least 2 hours until set firmly. Repeat with the remaining fruit, tinting the fondant with food colouring, if desired.

Frosted Fruits

To frost 4oz (100g) assorted fruits

4 ounces (100g) black and green grapes in pairs (or
  cherries, strawberries, Cape gooseberries,
  greengages, redcurrants or peeled lychees)
1 egg white
Caster sugar

Wash the fruit only if necessary and dry thoroughly on absorbent kitchen paper. Place the egg white in a small deep container and dip pairs of grapes in to coat all over. Shake off the surplus, then hold the grapes by the stalks over a sheet of greaseproof paper and sprinkle with sugar. Dip the bases in sugar then leave to dry for several hours in a warm dry place.

Chocolate-Coated Fruits

To coat 4oz (100g) assorted fruits

6 ounces (150g) white chocolate
6 ounces (150g) plain dessert chocolate
4 ounces (100g) assorted fruits (black and green
  grapes, cherries, strawberries, Cape gooseberries,
  greengages, peeled lychees, fresh dates, kumquats,
  orange segments, pineapple chunks or banana
  slices)
Food colouring (optional)

Grate the white and then the dark chocolate and place in separate small deep basins or cups. Heat a saucepan of water and remove from the heat. Place the basin with the white chocolate in the water and leave until the chocolate has melted. Avoid steam or water mixing with the chocolate.

Alternatively, melt in a microwave oven on defrost setting.

Dip the fruit in the chocolate and turn gently to let the excess fall off. Place on a dry plate and leave to set. Repeat with dark chocolate. Some fruits can be first dipped in white chocolate, left to set, then dipped in dark chocolate. If desired, the white chocolate can be tinted with food colouring.

When coating Cape gooseberries with chocolate, push the papery shells towards the stalk, before dipping the berries in the chocolate.

Filled Fruits

Cut and shape fruits to make containers for exotic mixtures to complement the flavour of the fruit. Citrus fruits with their firm skins make attractive baskets with handles. Softer fruits such as kiwi fruit, peaches, nectarines and bananas are best halved. Sections of orange and pineapple can be arranged around a firm filling to make an attractive basket. Fruits such as apples and pears that become brown when exposed to the air are not suitable for baskets, and peaches need to be used soon after preparing.

Fruits with Soft Centres

Makes 18 filled fruits

2 plums
2 small peaches
2 apricots
2 small nectarines
2 lychees
2 fresh dates
2 grapes
1 small apple
1 small pear
2 kumquats
1 quantity Spiced Nut Filling (above right)
1 quantity Orange Macaroon Filling (below right)
About 1/4 pint (125ml) orange juice
2 fluid ounces (50ml) double cream

Remove the stones from the plums, peaches, apricots, nectarines, lychees, dates and grapes. Peel and core the apples and pears.

Pile some filling into the centres of halved plums, peaches, apricots, nectarines, apples and pears. Press filling into the centres of the lychees, dates, grapes and kumquats and re-form the fruit.

Prepare a moderate oven at 375°F, 190°C, Gas Mark 5. Place the fruit in a shallow ovenproof dish and pour orange juice into the dish to cover the base. Bake in the centre of the oven until the fruit is just tender, 15 to 20 minutes. Test by piercing with a wooden cocktail stick.

Arrange the fruit on small plates and spoon a little juice around. Pour a little cream into the juice and swirl gently with a teaspoon. Serve hot or cold.

Spiced Nut Filling

To fill 9 assorted fruits

1 ounce (25g) ground almonds
1 ounce (25g) Toasted Hazelnuts*, finely chopped
1 ounce (25g) walnuts, finely chopped
1 ounce (25g) crystallized ginger, chopped
3 tablespoons (3 × 15ml spoons) mincemeat
2 tablespoons (2 × 15ml spoons) dark rum
1/2 teaspoon (1 × 2.5ml spoon) ground cinnamon
Finely grated rind of 1 lemon
1 egg yolk

Mix all the ingredients together and use to fill prepared fruits. Bake as directed under Fruits with Soft Centres.

Orange Macaroon Filling

To fill 9 assorted fruits

1 ounce (25g) butter
1 ounce (25g) icing sugar
1 egg yolk
1 teaspoon (1 × 5ml spoon) grated orange rind
1 tablespoon (1 × 15ml spoon) Grand Marnier liqueur
1 tablespoon (1 × 15ml spoon) orange juice
3 ounces (75g) macaroons, crushed

Cream the butter and sugar until light and fluffy. Beat in the egg yolk and orange rind, then the liqueur and orange juice a little at a time. Fold in the macaroons and leave for 5 minutes for the flavours to blend.

Use to fill the prepared fruits and bake as directed under Fruits with Soft Centres.

Citrus Fruit Basket

1 citrus fruit
1 quantity Marzipan or Cream Cheese Filling
  (opposite)

Use a felt pen to draw round the skin of a citrus fruit (kumquat, small orange, lime or lemon) half way from top to bottom, but leaving a ½in (1 cm) 'handle' across the top. With a sharp knife cut out the marked section a little away from the line to remove the section and the marking. Cut a small section off the base of the basket if it does not stand evenly on the plate. Gently cut out and scoop out the fruit, taking care to avoid damaging the handle. Press the removed fruit through a sieve and add the purée or juice to the filling ingredients. Pile the filling back into the basket.

Half Fruit Baskets

Use for kiwi fruit, bananas, tamarillos, apricots, peaches and nectarines. Cut the fruit in half, remove stones or seeds as appropriate, and cut a little fruit off each end if necessary for the halves to sit firmly on the plate. Carefully cut round the edges, leaving a thin 'wall' to hold the fruit firmly.
  Press the removed fruit through a nylon sieve and mix with Marzipan or Cream Cheese Filling.

Marzipan Filling

Fills about 4oz (100g) fruit

1 ounce (25g) ground almonds
1 ounce (25g) icing sugar
1 teaspoon (1 × 5ml spoon) egg white
2 teaspoons (2 × 5ml spoons) brandy
A few drops almond extract
Cake crumbs

Mix the ingredients, together with the purée or juice from the fruit baskets, and add sufficient cake crumbs to make the mixture firm enough to handle.

Cream Cheese Filling

Fills about 4oz (100g) fruit

1 ounce (25g) butter
1 ounce (25g) icing sugar
2 ounces (50g) full fat soft cheese
1 tablespoon (1 × 15ml spoon) cognac
Cake crumbs

Cream butter and sugar together until soft and fluffy. Beat in the soft cheese, cognac and fruit juice or purée from the baskets. Add sufficient cake crumbs to make the mixture firm enough to handle.

Kissels

These mixtures of softly set fruits are called Kissels in Eastern Europe, Red Fruit Pudding in Scandinavia and Red Grits in northern Germany. Serve these clear, bright desserts in elegant glasses and top with soft cream if desired.

Rhubarb and Orange Kissel

6 portions in 4 fl oz (100ml) glasses

½ pound (200g) champagne rhubarb
4 ounces (100g) granulated sugar
2 tablespoons (2 × 15ml spoons) water
1 orange
2 teaspoons (2 × 5ml spoons) arrowroot
2 tablespoons (2 × 15ml spoons) dry sherry
1 teaspoon (1 × 5ml spoon) caster sugar
2 fluid ounces (50ml) lightly whipped cream

Trim the rhubarb and cut into ½in (1.25cm) pieces. In a medium pan, dissolve the sugar in the water.

Pare two strips of orange and add to the syrup. Bring to boil and add the rhubarb; return to boil, turn off the heat, cover and leave for 10 minutes.
  Cut another strip of orange rind and shred finely; reserve for decoration. Use a serrated knife to cut the remaining peel and pith off the orange. Cut out the segments and add to the pan. Blend the arrowroot with the sherry and add to the fruit. Bring to boil, stirring. Add more sugar, if desired. Cool and pour into four glasses. Sprinkle caster sugar over each, then chill.
  Pour on the cream and decorate with reserved orange shreds.

Red Fruit Kissel

4 portions in 4 fl oz (100ml) glasses

2 ounces (50g) blackcurrants
2 ounces (50g) redcurrants
¼ pint (125ml) water
2 ounces (50g) muscovado light brown sugar
1 cinnamon stick
2 ounces (50g) loganberries
2 ounces (50g) wild strawberries
2 teaspoons (2 × 5ml spoons) arrowroot
1 tablespoon (1 × 15ml spoon) cherry brandy
1 teaspoon (1 × 5ml spoon) caster sugar

Remove the stalks from the blackcurrants and redcurrants and place in a small saucepan with the water, sugar and cinnamon. Bring to boil, cover and cook 2 minutes. Add the loganberries and strawberries and bring to boil; remove the cinnamon stick. Blend the arrowroot with the cherry brandy, add to the fruit and bring to boil, stirring. Stir gently until cooked, then pour into four small glasses. Sprinkle the surface with sugar and leave to cool. Serve chilled.

Golden Fruit Kissel

6 portions 4 fl oz (100ml) glasses

4 golden plums
4 apricots
4 kumquats, sliced
¼ pint (125ml) sweet white wine
2 ounces (50g) peeled mango
2 teaspoons (2 × 5ml spoons) arrowroot
2 ounces (50g) golden granulated sugar
2 tablespoons (2 × 15ml spoons) Amaretto liqueur
1 teaspoon (1 × 5ml spoon) caster sugar
2 fluid ounces (50ml) soured cream

Cut the plums and apricots in halves and remove the stones. Chop the fruit, then place in a small saucepan with the kumquats and wine, bring to boil, cover and simmer 5 minutes. Remove 6 kumquat slices and reserve for decoration. Cut the mango into small cubes and add.

Blend the arrowroot with the sugar and liqueur. Add to the fruit mixture, bring to boil, stirring. Remove from heat and cool. Pour into six small glasses, sprinkle with caster sugar and leave to cool.

To serve, beat soured cream and pour over the surface. Decorate each with a kumquat slice.

Spiced Blackberry and Apple Kissel

6 portions in 4 fl oz (100ml) glasses

6 fl oz (150ml) apple juice
1 vanilla pod
1 cinnamon stick
2 cloves
1½ in (1.25cm) piece fresh ginger, grated
1 cooking apple, peeled, cored and chopped
4 ounces (100g) blackberries
2 ounces (50g) muscovado light brown sugar
2 teaspoons (2 × 5ml spoon) arrowroot or cornflour
2 tablespoons (2 × 15ml spoons) cognac
1 teaspoon (1 × 5ml spoon) caster sugar
2 fl oz (50ml) double cream
6 slices dessert apple
1 teaspoon (1 × 5ml spoon) lemon juice

Place the apple juice in a small saucepan and add the vanilla pod, cinnamon stick, cloves and ginger. Bring to boil, cover and leave to infuse 10 minutes. Strain and return the juice to the saucepan. Add the apple, blackberries and brown sugar. Bring to boil, cover and cook about 2 minutes, until the fruit is tender but whole.

Blend the arrowroot or cornflour with the brandy and add to the fruit. Bring to boil, stirring gently. Cool slightly then pour into six glasses. Sprinkle caster sugar over the surface. Cool, then chill.

To serve, whip the cream until it just holds its shape and pour over the fruit. Decorate each glass with a slice of apple, first brushed with lemon juice to prevent browning.

Flambéed Fruits

Before starting to flambé, collect all the ingredients, cut them into small bite-sized pieces and arrange them attractively on a tray. The fruits are then fried, and turned in a light caramel sauce; liqueur is added and flamed to concentrate the flavour and release the alcohol. Serve immediately. Firm fruits such as pineapple, banana, peaches, nectarines, apricots, cherries and pears are best. Use a spirit or fondue bourguignonne heater, and an attractive copper frying pan; and remember that the pieces of fruit must be at room temperature for successful flambéing.

Flambéed Fruit

4 portions

About 6 ounces (150g) prepared fruit
1 ounce (25g) butter
2 ounces (50g) granulated sugar
1 teaspoon (1 × 5ml spoon) orange rind
Juice of 1 small orange and 1 lemon
1 tablespoon (1 × 15ml spoon) liqueur
2 teaspoons (2 × 5ml spoons) spirit

Quickly fry the fruit in half the melted butter; remove from the pan and keep warm. Add the remaining butter and sugar to the pan and stir over a low heat until the sugar has turned golden brown. Add the orange and lemon juices and the rind and stir to dissolve the caramel. Cook over high heat for about 1 minute until the sauce thickens.

   Return the fruit to the pan and heat. Pour over the liqueur and spirit, ignite and leave the flames to die down before spooning some fruit and sauce on to serving plates.

Ingredients, sauces, edible containers, etc that are asterisked in the recipes on these pages are given in detail on pages 147 to 156. For exact page numbers, refer to the index at the end of the book.

Fruits

Pineapple
Cut one ring for each portion from a fresh pineapple. Use Cointreau and dark rum.

Banana
Half a banana is sufficient for each portion; cut in diagonal slices. Use Malibu and white rum.

Peaches
Use fresh peaches, if possible, and allow half per portion. Cut the fruit in slices and use Grand Marnier and brandy.

Nectarines
Serve half per portion, cut in slices. Use Benedictine and brandy.

Apricots
Serve one apricot per portion, cut in half. Use Amaretto and brandy.

Cherries
Use morello cherries and replace the orange juice with 4 tablespoons (4 × 15ml spoons) red wine and add 1 tablespoon (1 × 15ml spoon) redcurrant jelly. Use kirsch and brandy.

Pears
Serve half a ripe pear for each portion; peel and cut in thick slices. Use Galliano and vodka.

Batters, Deep-Fried Desserts

Doughnuts, crêpes, fritters, waffles and delicious confections made from potato pastry and even bread are included in this chapter. Fry them quickly, at the correct temperature, to make sure they absorb as little oil as possible. All can be served with a variety of fillings and accompaniments.

Doughnuts

Traditional doughnuts are made with a rich yeast mixture, but these are deliciously 'short' textured. The basic recipe can be adapted to make delicious honey cakes.

American Doughnuts

Ten 2in (5cm) doughnuts

3 ounces (75g) self-raising flour
1 ounce (25g) caster sugar
1 ounce (25g) margarine
2 tablespoons (2 × 15ml spoons) beaten egg
1 tablespoon (1 × 15ml spoon) milk
Caster sugar

Prepare a deep-fat fryer and heat oil to 370°F (185°C).

Place flour and sugar in a medium bowl. Add margarine, cut up, and rub in until it resembles fine breadcrumbs. Add egg and sufficient milk to make a smooth dough. Knead lightly on a floured surface. Roll out to ¼in (5mm) thickness. Using a 2in (5cm) cutter, cut out the doughnuts, then use a 1¼in (3cm) cutter to remove the centres.

Fry doughnuts about 2 minutes or until golden brown on both sides. Drain on kitchen paper and coat with caster sugar. Serve warm or cold.

Almond and Honey Balls

Ten 2in (5cm) balls

1 ounce (25g) ground almonds
½ teaspoon (1 × 2.5ml spoon) almond extract
1 quantity American Doughnut recipe, uncooked

Syrup
3 rounded tablespoons (6 × 15ml spoons) clear honey
1 tablespoon (1 × 15ml spoon) lemon juice
1 tablespoon (1 × 15ml spoon) dark rum
1 tablespoon (1 × 15ml spoon) Toasted Chopped Almonds*

To serve
6 tablespoons (6 × 15ml spoons) Greek yoghurt
10 small pieces of honeycomb

Mix the ground almonds and extract into the dough and use extra milk, if necessary, to make a soft dough. Drop teaspoonfuls of the mixture on to a lightly floured surface and gently roll to make neat balls. Fry in a deep-fat fryer for 3 to 4 minutes until deep golden brown. Drain on kitchen paper. Place balls in a small bowl.

To make the syrup, gently warm the honey, lemon juice and rum. Stir in the nuts. Pour syrup over balls and turn them over several times to coat. They can be served warm or cold.

To serve, spread a tablespoon (15ml spoon) of yoghurt on a plate and place an Almond and Honey Ball on top. Decorate the plate with a piece of honeycomb.

Previous pages, clockwise from left *Maple and Vanilla Waffle (page 108); Mincemeat Curls (page 109); Peaches and Praline Cream crêpe (page 112); 2in (5cm) Almond and Honey Ball (right); American Doughnuts (above).*

> **Perfect frying**
> Do not allow the fat to get too hot or the outside will become overcooked before the inside is set.

Chocolate Surprises

Four 2in (5cm) filled doughnuts

½ quantity American Doughnut recipe, uncooked
4 pieces thin dessert chocolate
Icing sugar, to coat
1 teaspoon (1 × 5ml spoon) kirsch
About 16 canned orange segments

Roll out the dough to ⅛in (6mm) thickness and cut out four circles using a 3in (7.5cm) cutter. Place a piece of chocolate in the centre of each. Brush the outside edge of each circle with water and draw up to enclose the chocolate; seal well. Turn the doughnut over with the join underneath and gently flatten with a rolling pin to a 2in (5cm) round (or smaller if the chocolate begins to show through).

Fry doughnuts in a deep-fat fryer for 2 minutes or until golden brown. Drain on kitchen paper. Sprinkle the doughnuts liberally with sifted icing sugar.

Sprinkle kirsch over the orange segments and toss lightly. Place each doughnut on a plate and arrange the orange segments around it. Serve at once.

Cinnamon Doughnuts

Five 2in (5cm) doughnuts

½ quantity American Doughnut recipe
2 teaspoons (2 × 5ml spoons) caster sugar
½ teaspoon (1 × 2.5ml spoon) ground cinnamon
Whipped cream with rum
5 strawberries

Prepare doughnuts as recipe and drain on kitchen paper.

Mix sugar and cinnamon together in a bag and lightly toss the doughnuts in it.

Pipe a large rosette of cream in the centre of each doughnut and top with a strawberry. Serve at once.

Orange Syrup Cakes

Six 2in (5cm) cakes

1 quantity American Doughnut recipe made with 2 ounces (50g) semolina to replace 1 ounce (25g) of the flour. Omit the milk and add 1 tablespoon (1 × 15ml spoon) orange juice, grated rind of half an orange and ½ teaspoon (1 × 2.5ml spoon) ground cinnamon to the mixture

Syrup
4 ounces (100g) granulated sugar
3 tablespoons (3 × 15ml spoons) orange juice
¼ pint (125ml) water

To serve
2 tablespoons (2 × 15ml spoons) Greek yoghurt
Glazed Orange Peel Strands*

Divide the dough into six and lightly knead each piece into a 2in (5cm) long fat bolster shape. Fry in a deep-fat fryer for 3 to 4 minutes until deep golden brown. Drain on kitchen paper and place the cakes in a small bowl.

To make the syrup, place the sugar, orange juice and water in a small saucepan and stir over a low heat until the sugar has dissolved. Increase heat and boil rapidly until the liquid has been reduced by half. Pour the syrup over the orange cakes and turn them over carefully. They can be served warm or cold.

To serve, spread a little yoghurt on a small plate and place an Orange Syrup Cake on top. Sprinkle Glazed Orange Peel Strands on each and spoon any remaining syrup over the top.

To freeze
Orange Syrup Cakes can be frozen. When cold, remove from the syrup and place in a small freezer container. Allow to defrost slowly at room temperature.

Lemon Poppy Sticks
with Cranberry Cream

Five 1½in (4cm) doughnuts

*1 teaspoon (1 × 5ml spoon) grated lemon
   rind*
2 teaspoons (2 × 5ml spoons) poppy seeds
*½ quantity American Doughnut recipe (page 104),
   uncooked*
2 teaspoons (2 × 5ml spoons) Vanilla Sugar*
3 pieces dessert chocolate
3 fluid ounces (75ml) double cream
3 tablespoons (3 × 15ml spoons) Cranberry Sauce*

Mix lemon rind and 1 teaspoon (5ml spoon) poppy
seeds into the dough. Divide the mixture into five
pieces and roll each into a 1½in (4cm) sausage
shape.

Fry doughnuts in a deep-fat fryer for 2 minutes
until golden brown on all sides. Drain on kitchen
paper. Toss them in the reserved poppy seeds and
Vanilla Sugar, to coat.

Melt chocolate in a small basin over hot water (or
in a microwave oven) and dip both ends of each
doughnut in chocolate; leave to set.

Whip the cream until stiff. Fold in 2 tablespoons
(2 × 15ml spoons) Cranberry Sauce. Place a large
swirl of cream on each serving plate, top with a little
Cranberry Sauce and place the doughnut on
one side.

Waffles

These crisp, wafer-like waffles are served with luscious sweet toppings. Make
them in advance, store in the freezer, and reheat under a hot grill or in a toaster.
Prepare the topping before making the waffles.

Crispy Waffles

Twelve 2½in (6cm) waffles

3 ounces (75g) flour
Pinch of salt
1½ teaspoons (3 × 2.5ml spoons) baking powder
2 tablespoons (2 × 15ml spoons) sugar
1 egg, separated
1 tablespoon (1 × 15ml spoon) melted butter
¼ pint (125ml) milk
Knob of butter for cooking

Sift flour, salt and baking powder into a medium
bowl. Add the sugar, beaten egg yolk, butter and
milk and beat until smooth.

Alternatively, place all these ingredients in a
liquidizer or food processor and run machine until
batter is smooth.

Thoroughly butter a waffle iron and heat slowly
for 5 minutes. Whisk egg white until stiff, and fold
into batter.

Pour 1 rounded tablespoon (15ml spoon) batter
into centre of lower half of iron until it spreads to
within 1in (2.5cm) of the edge.

Close and cook for about 1 minute, turning if
necessary, until the waffle is golden brown and
releases easily from the iron.

Serve the waffles hot with any of the following
toppings.

Ingredients, sauces, edible containers, etc
that are asterisked in the recipes on these
pages are given in detail on pages 147 to
156. For exact page numbers, refer to the
index at the end of the book.

Left *Pentland Plum (page 109).*

Lemon Waffles

Six 2½in (6cm) waffles

½ quantity Crispy Waffles recipe (page 107)
1 teaspoon (1 × 5ml spoon) grated lemon rind

Stir lemon rind into batter and cook as directed.

Peach Melba

Six 2½in (6cm) waffles

6 Lemon Waffles, as recipe
6 scoops Peach Sorbet (page 140)
A few drops almond extract
6 tablespoons (6 × 15ml spoons) Chantilly Cream
(page 122)
2 tablespoons (2 × 15ml spoons) Cranberry Sauce*

Place each waffle on a small plate. Top with a scoop of Peach Sorbet.

Stir almond extract into the Chantilly Cream and swirl 1 tablespoon (15ml spoon) on to each sorbet. Top with a teaspoonful (5ml spoon) of Cranberry Sauce. Serve at once.

Banana and Chocolate Secrets

Six 2½in (6cm) waffles

6 Crispy Waffles, as recipe (page 107)
3 large ripe bananas
6 teaspoons (6 × 5ml spoons) dark rum
6 tablespoons (6 × 15ml spoons) Hot Chocolate
Sauce*
6 tablespoons (6 × 15ml spoons) whipped cream
12 Marzipan Leaves*

Place each waffle on a serving plate. Peel and halve the bananas, then slice them thinly and spread each half across one waffle, keeping a banana shape. Sprinkle rum over the bananas before covering with Hot Chocolate Sauce.

Pipe a line of cream along the top and decorate each with 2 Marzipan Leaves. Serve immediately.

Apricot Drop Scones

Six 2½in (6cm) drop scones

Oil for greasing
½ quantity Crispy Waffle recipe (page 107)
3 fresh apricots (or 6 canned apricot halves)
2 ounces (50g) sugar
3 fluid ounces (75ml) white wine
2 teaspoons (2 × 5ml spoons) brandy
6 tablespoons (6 × 15ml spoons) Chantilly
Cream (page 122)
Chopped pistachio nuts

Lightly grease a griddle pan or heavy-based frying pan. Drop a dessertspoonful (10ml spoon) of batter on to the pan and cook 1 minute each side or until deep golden brown in colour.

Keep warm in a clean tea towel over a pan of hot water.

Halve apricots and remove stones (drain apricots if canned). Place sugar and wine in a small pan. Bring to boil. Add apricot halves, reduce heat and simmer for 2 to 3 minutes. Remove apricots with a slotted spoon. Add brandy to the pan and cook syrup gently until it coats the back of the spoon.

Place an apricot half on each drop scone and drizzle some syrup over the fruit. Pipe small rosettes of Chantilly Cream around the edges of the scones and sprinkle pistachio nuts over the dessert.

Maple and Vanilla Waffles

Six 2½in (5cm) waffles

6 Crispy Waffles, as recipe (page 107)
6 tiny scoops Vanilla Ice Cream (page 136)
4 tablespoons (4 × 15ml spoons) maple syrup
6 teaspoons (6 × 5ml spoons) Toasted
Chopped Almonds*

Place each waffle on a serving plate. Place a scoop of ice cream on top and coat with maple syrup. Sprinkle nuts over syrup.

Note: Use a heart-shaped waffle iron if you have one.

Potato Pastry

Potato pastry, an Austrian speciality, makes a wonderfully soft crust for
sweet dishes.

Soft Potato Pastry

16 portions

12 ounces (300g) large potatoes
1 ounce (25g) butter
1½ ounces (40g) semolina
1 egg yolk
3-4 ounces (75-100g) flour
1 teaspoon (1 × 5ml spoon) baking powder
¼ teaspoon salt

Scrub potatoes and bake in a hot oven until soft.
Scoop out the flesh and sieve into a basin. Add
butter, semolina, eggs, half the flour, the baking
powder and the salt. Beat ingredients together until
smooth. Gradually add sufficient flour to make a soft
dough. Knead lightly on a well-floured surface.
Cover pastry and leave in the refrigerator for 20
minutes.

Pentland Plums

6 covered plums

Oil for deep frying
6 small red plums
3 ounces (75g) marzipan
½ quantity Soft Potato Pastry recipe
2 ounces (50g) fresh white breadcrumbs
2 teaspoons (2 × 5ml spoons) sherry
4 rounded tablespoons (8 × 15ml spoons) sieved
*   apricot purée, using fresh or dried apricots*

Prepare a deep-fat fryer and heat oil to 370°F
(185°C). Cut two-thirds of the way round each plum
and remove the stones. Divide marzipan into six
pieces and use to fill the cavity in each plum.
    Remove pastry from refrigerator and lightly
knead on a well-floured surface until smooth.
Divide into six equal pieces, flatten and mould each
one round a plum to cover evenly. Roll in
breadcrumbs, pressing them on lightly. Deep-fry
plums 4 to 5 minutes until golden brown, turning
them over during cooking. Make sure that the fat is
not too hot or the outside will become too dark
before the plum is soft. Drain on kitchen paper and
keep warm. Serve with apricot sauce made by
beating the sherry into the apricot purée.

Mincemeat Curls

Six 3in (7.5cm) curls

Oil for deep frying
½ quantity Soft Potato Pastry recipe
2 tablespoons (2 × 15ml spoons) sesame seeds
3 tablespoons (3 × 15ml spoons) mincemeat

To serve
6 Marzipan Leaves*
3 cherries, halved
Brandy Cream (page 122)

Prepare a deep-fat fryer and heat oil to 370°F
(185°C).
    Lightly knead the pastry until smooth on a
well-floured surface. Sprinkle sesame seeds lightly
over this surface and place pastry on top. Roll out
pastry ¼in (6mm) thick and cut out six 3in (7.5cm)
circles.
    Place a teaspoon (5ml spoon) mincemeat in the
centre of each. Brush the edges with water and fold
pastry in half over the filling. Seal edges and snip
with scissors at ¼in (5mm) intervals. Pull ends
gently away from curve to form a horseshoe.
    Deep-fry 2 to 3 minutes until golden brown.
Drain on kitchen paper and keep warm.
    To serve, decorate with a Marzipan Leaf and half a
cherry. Serve with Brandy Cream.

Ingredients, sauces, edible containers, etc
that are asterisked in the recipes on these
pages are given in detail on pages 147 to
156. For exact page numbers, refer to the
index at the end of the book.

Crêpes

Fine, lacy crêpes can be folded, rolled or formed into cones to make delicious containers for a variety of fillings. Make them in advance and store in the refrigerator or freezer.

Mini-Crêpes

Twenty 3in (7.5cm) crêpes

2 ounces (50g) flour
Pinch of salt
1 egg, beaten
2½ fluid ounces (65ml) milk
4 tablespoons (4 × 15ml spoons) water
1 tablespoon (1 × 15ml spoon) brandy
Knob butter or lard for frying

Sift flour and salt together in a medium bowl. Mix egg, milk, water and brandy together and gradually beat into the flour to make a smooth batter. Alternatively, liquidize all the ingredients together until smooth.

Heat a small crêpe pan, griddle or heavy-based frying pan and brush with butter or lard. Using a dessertspoon (10ml spoon) place a spoonful of the batter in the pan and quickly and lightly spread out to a 3in (7.5cm) circle with the back of the spoon. Repeat to make more mini-crêpes in the pan. Fry for about one minute until set, then flip over and cook for 30 seconds until the second side is golden brown. Slide the crêpes on to a plate placed over a pan of hot water and cook the remaining batter.

Variations
Each of the following recipes makes ten 3in (7.5cm) crêpes

Chocolate Crêpes
Sprinkle 1½ teaspoons (1½ × 5ml spoons) cocoa powder and 1 teaspoon (1 × 5ml spoon) caster sugar over the surface of batter made with ½ quantity Mini-Crêpes recipe. Leave a few seconds before beating or liquidizing.

Orange Crêpes
Stir 2 teaspoons (2 × 5ml spoons) finely grated orange rind into batter made with ½ quantity Mini-Crêpes recipe.

Cinnamon Crêpes
Stir ½ teaspoon (1 × 2.5ml spoon) ground cinnamon into batter made with ½ quantity Mini-Crêpes recipe.

Coconut Crêpes
Stir 1 teaspoon (1 × 5ml spoon) desiccated coconut into batter made with ½ quantity Mini-Crêpes recipe.

Freezing crêpes
Stack between pieces of greaseproof paper or freezer film. Place stack in a plastic bag and freeze for up to six weeks. Thaw at room temperature and re-heat over hot water or in a microwave oven.

Right *Selection of crêpes, on black plate from left: Raspberries au Fromage (page 112); Chocolate and Nut (page 112); Banana with Butterscotch Sauce (page 113).*

Peaches and Praline Cream

Ten 3in (7.5cm) filled crêpes

1 tablespoon (1 × 15ml spoon) orange juice
1 teaspoon (1 × 5ml spoon) sugar
1 peach, peeled, stoned and roughly chopped
1 tablespoon (1 × 15ml spoon) brandy
1 ounce (25g) Praline*
2 fluid ounces (50ml) double cream, lightly
* whipped*
10 Mini-Crêpes, as recipe (page 110)

Heat the orange juice with the sugar in a small pan, add the peach and cook for 2 to 3 minutes. Strain through a sieve and reserve both fruit and juice. Stir the brandy into the juice and heat gently.

Fold the crushed Praline into the cream and divide between the crêpes. Place the blanched peach on the cream and fold the crêpes over. Sprinkle the orange juice mixture over the surface.

Raspberries au Fromage

Ten 3in (7.5cm) filled crêpes

2 tablespoons (2 × 15ml spoons) soured fresh
* cream*
2 ounces (50g) soft white cheese or sieved cottage
* cheese*
1 tablespoon (1 × 15ml spoon) icing sugar
3 ounces (75g) raspberries
10 Mini-Crêpes, as recipe (page 110)
1 tablespoon (1 × 15ml spoon) sieved icing sugar

Beat the soured cream into the cheese until smooth. Beat in the icing sugar.

Reserve a few raspberries for decoration and fold remainder into cheese mixture.

Fold the crêpes in half and fill with the raspberry cheese. Dust the top of the crêpes with sieved icing sugar and serve with a few extra raspberries placed around them.

Successful cooking
When placing batter in the hot pan, use a quick, light-handed circular movement to ensure even spreading. Cook two or three crêpes together.

Chocolate and Nut

Ten 3in (7.5cm) filled crêpes

1 egg yolk
2 teaspoons (2 × 5ml spoons) Vanilla Sugar*
2 teaspoons (2 × 5ml spoons) cornflour
4 fluid ounces (100ml) milk
2 squares plain chocolate, chopped
1 egg white
1 ounce (25g) caster sugar
1 ounce (25g) mixed nuts, finely chopped
1 ounce (25g) macaroons, coarsely crushed
3 tablespoons (3 × 15ml spoons) double cream
1 tablespoon (1 × 15ml spoon) brandy
10 Mini-Crêpes, as recipe (page 110)

Blend the egg yolk, Vanilla Sugar and cornflour together in a small bowl. Bring the milk to the boil then stir into the egg yolk mixture. Pour into a small saucepan and cook, stirring, over a low heat, until the mixture thickens.

Meanwhile, melt the chocolate in a bowl placed over a pan of hot water, then stir into the custard.

Whisk the egg white until stiff. Gradually whisk in the sugar. Fit a small piping bag with a small star tube and fill with meringue.

Prepare a medium-hot grill.

Mix the nuts, macaroons, cream and brandy into the chocolate custard and divide the mixture between the crêpes. Fold them over. Place on a baking sheet and pipe a pattern of meringue over the surface of each crêpe. Place under the grill until lightly browned.

Walnut Ice Cream and Maple Syrup

Ten 3in (7.5cm) filled crêpes

3 fluid ounces (75ml) double cream, chilled
1 ounce (25g) brown sugar
1 ounce (25g) walnuts, very finely chopped
10 Chocolate Crêpes (page 110)
3 tablespoons (3 × 15ml spoons) maple syrup

Whip the cream with the brown sugar until it stands in soft peaks. Fold in the nuts then spoon into a shallow metal container, cover and place in the freezer or the top of the refrigerator until firm.

Prepare the crêpes, then place small scoops of the frozen walnut mixture in the centre of each one. Fold the crêpes over. Trickle maple syrup over each. Serve at once.

Ground Almond and Curaçao

Ten 3in (7.5cm) filled crêpes

10 Cinnamon Crêpes (page 110)
1 ounce (25g) caster sugar
1 ounce (25g) butter, softened
1 ounce (25g) ground almonds
1 teaspoon (1 × 5ml spoon) curaçao
Knob of clarified butter
2 tablespoons (2 × 15ml spoons) Toasted
  Flaked Almonds*
4 orange segments, pith and peel removed, chopped

Sauce
2 tablespoons (2 × 15ml spoons) orange curaçao
2 tablespoons (2 × 15ml spoons) brandy

Prepare the crêpes. Work the sugar, butter, ground almonds and curaçao together with a fork. Place down the centre of the crêpes and fold over into rectangular parcels.

Heat the crêpe pan gently, then wipe around the inside with clarified butter. Place the crêpe parcels, seam-side down, in the pan.

To make the sauce, warm the curaçao and brandy in a ladle, ignite with a taper then pour over the crêpes. Serve immediately sprinkled with chopped orange segments and the Toasted Flaked Almonds.

To assist your timetable
Ground Almond and Curaçao filling can be prepared in advance. Wrap and keep in the refrigerator for up to 4 hours.

Keeping crêpes warm
Stack them on a plate over a pan of hot water and cover with a clean tea towel.

Banana with Butterscotch Sauce

Ten 3in (7.5cm) filled crêpes

10 Orange Crêpes (page 110)
1 banana
2 teaspoons (2 × 5ml spoons) lemon juice
½ ounce (15g) butter
2 teaspoons (2 × 5ml spoons) brown sugar

Sauce
1 ounce (25g) butter
1 ounce (25g) soft brown sugar
3 tablespoons (3 × 15ml spoons) cream

Prepare the crêpes and keep warm.
Peel and slice the banana then sprinkle with lemon juice.

Melt the butter in a small non-stick frying pan then stir in the brown sugar and heat gently until the sugar has dissolved. Add the banana and cook on a low heat for 2 to 3 minutes.

Melt the butter for the sauce in a small non-stick saucepan. Stir in the sugar and heat gently until it has dissolved. Boil for 2 minutes, stirring constantly. Remove from the heat. Cool slightly then stir in the cream. Divide the banana mixture between the crêpes, then fold them over. Place on warmed plates and trickle the sauce over.

Rum and Pineapple

Ten 3in (7.5cm) filled crêpes

10 Coconut Crêpes (page 110)
2 ounces (50g) peeled fresh pineapple, chopped
3 tablespoons (3 × 15ml spoons) dark rum
2 tablespoons (2 × 15ml spoons) sweet sherry
1 teaspoon (1 × 5ml spoon) cornflour
1 teaspoon (1 × 5ml spoon) sugar
1 tablespoon (1 × 15ml spoon) icing sugar

Prepare the crêpes and keep warm.
Marinate the pineapple in the rum and sherry in a basin for 10 minutes. Blend cornflour in a small saucepan with 1 tablespoon (1 × 15ml spoon) water then stir in the pineapple and liquid and sugar. Bring to boil, stirring.

Divide the pineapple between the crêpes and fold them over. Place spoonfuls of the rum sauce on warmed plates and place the crêpes on top. Dredge with icing sugar.

Windsor Slices

These delectable desserts, made from bread coated with egg and then fried, are a sweet variation on French toast. They taste especially good served with fruit or ice cream.

Windsor Slices

Six 2in (5cm) circles

*Three ¼in (5mm) thick day-old slices
    white bread
1 egg
Pinch of cinnamon
3 fluid ounces (75ml) white wine
3 tablespoons (3 × 15ml spoons)
    caster sugar
1 ounce (25g) butter*

Using a 2in (5cm) cutter, cut out two circles from each slice of bread.

Beat egg, cinnamon, wine and 2 tablespoons (2 × 15ml spoons) sugar together in a basin.

Heat butter in a small, heavy-based pan. Dip bread into egg mixture, lift out and fry 1 or 2 minutes on each side until golden brown. Toss bread in remaining sugar and serve hot with a choice of toppings.

Strawberry Cups

Six 2in (5cm) cups

*6 cooked Windsor Slices, as recipe
9 large, firm strawberries
2 tablespoons (2 × 15ml spoons) kirsch
1 egg white
2 ounces (50g) caster sugar*

Prepare a medium-hot grill. Place the Windsor Slices on an oven-proof plate.

Remove hulls from strawberries and cut each strawberry in half, lengthways. Place in a basin and sprinkle with kirsch.

Whisk egg white until stiff, then fold in the sugar. Place meringue in a piping bag fitted with a small star tube. Pipe a thick ring of meringue round the edge of each Windsor Slice. Place them under a medium-hot grill until the meringue is lightly browned.

Arrange 3 strawberry halves in each and drizzle kirsch over. Serve at once.

Apricot Alaskas

Six 2in (5cm) alaskas

*6 Windsor Slices as recipe, but made with beer
    instead of wine and with bread cut into 2in (5cm)
    squares
2 ounces (50g) dried apricots, soaked
    overnight
2 tablespoons (2 × 15ml spoons) brandy
2 tablespoons (2 × 15ml spoons) beer
2 egg whites
4 ounces (100g) caster sugar
6 small scoops Vanilla Ice Cream
    (page 136)
18 small pieces angelica*

Prepare a medium-hot grill. Arrange the Windsor Slices on an oven-proof dish.

Liquidize the apricots, brandy and beer together until smooth. Divide between the fried slices.

Whisk egg whites until thick; gradually whisk in the sugar. Place meringue in a piping bag with a small star tube.

Arrange a scoop of ice cream on top of the purée and cover completely with swirls of meringue. Place alaskas under a medium-hot grill until golden brown.

Serve the alaskas at once, each decorated with 3 pieces of angelica.

Right, from left *Kumquat Fritters (page 116); Frosted Grapes (page 97); Fondue Fritters (page 116); Maraschino Cherry Fritters (page 116); 1¼in (3cm) Rich Secret Dessert (page 117).*

Fritters

Firm, tangy fruits are dipped in a light batter and deep-fried until crisp and golden in colour. The coating helps to protect them from the heat and flavour of the oil.

Fruit Fritters

Twelve 1in (2.5cm) fritters

Batter
2 ounces (50g) flour
Pinch of salt
2½ fluid ounces (65ml) water
2 heaped tablespoons (4 × 15ml spoons) stiffly whipped egg white

Oil for deep frying
12 pieces of fruit, eg grapes, kumquats, apple pieces, cherries, strawberries, damsons

To make the batter, sift flour and salt into a bowl. Make a well in the centre and add water. Beat until smooth. Leave batter to rest for 30 minutes. Just before using, carefully fold in the egg white with a metal spoon.

Prepare a deep-fat fryer and heat oil to 370°F (185°C). Dip pieces of fruit in the batter, shake off excess and place the fruit into the hot fat, only a few pieces at a time. Make sure the oil returns to the correct temperature before each new addition of fruit. Fry 3 to 4 minutes until golden brown, turning them over half way through cooking. Drain the fritters on kitchen paper and keep warm while frying the remaining pieces.

Fondue Fritters

Twelve 1in (2.5cm) fritters

3 ounces (75g) Stilton
1 quantity batter from Fruit Fritters recipe, using rind and juice of one large orange in place of water

To serve
3 tablespoons (3 × 15ml spoons) caraway seeds
About 24 Frosted Grapes (page 97)

Cut cheese into 12 squares and dip in batter. Deep-fry for 2 to 3 minutes until golden brown. Drain on kitchen paper, toss in caraway seeds to coat, and keep warm. Serve with Frosted Grapes.

Kumquat Fritters

Twelve 1in (2.5cm) fritters

12 kumquats
1 quantity batter from Fruit Fritters recipe
2 tablespoons (2 × 15ml spoons) icing sugar

Sauce
2 teaspoons (2 × 5ml spoons) brandy
Grated rind of ½ lemon
2 fluid ounces (50ml) warmed sieved marmalade

Dip the kumquats in the batter and deep-fry for 1 minute, then remove from oil and re-dip in batter. Fry the fritters for 2 to 3 minutes until golden brown. Drain on kitchen paper and keep warm.

Sift icing sugar over fritters before serving.

To make the sauce, stir the brandy and lemon rind into the sieved marmalade in a small pan and heat through gently. Serve each fritter with a small spoonful of sauce.

Ginger Nuggets

Twelve 1in (2.5cm) fritters

12 nuggets of stem ginger in syrup
1 quantity batter from Fruit Fritters recipe
Caster sugar to coat

Ginger sauce
2 tablespoons (2 × 15ml spoons) syrup from the ginger jar
6 tablespoons (6 × 15ml spoons) thickly set Greek yoghurt or soured cream

Dip nuggets of ginger in the batter. Deep-fry for 1 minute then remove and re-dip in the batter. Fry fritters for 2 to 3 minutes until golden brown. Drain on kitchen paper and keep warm.

Toss in caster sugar to coat.

To make the sauce, gradually add syrup to the yoghurt or soured cream, stirring continuously. Serve each fritter with a spoonful of sauce.

Brandied Apple Fritters

Twelve 1in (2.5cm) fritters

1½ small sweet, firm apples
3 tablespoons (3 × 15ml spoons) brandy
2 tablespoons (2 × 15ml spoons) demerara sugar
½ teaspoon (1 × 2.5ml spoons) cinnamon
1 quantity batter from Fruit Fritters recipe
Vanilla Sugar* or desiccated coconut to coat

To serve
4 tablespoons (4 × 15ml spoons) whipped cream
Warmed, sieved Cranberry Sauce*
12 Frosted Mint Leaves*

Halve, quarter, peel and core the apples. Cut each quarter into two pieces. Place brandy, demerara sugar and cinnamon in a medium basin, add apples and toss, to coat. Leave 20 minutes turning occasionally. Drain apples on kitchen paper. Reserve liquid.

Dip apples in batter and deep-fry 3 to 4 minutes until golden brown. Drain on kitchen paper and keep warm. Toss in Vanilla Sugar or desiccated coconut, to coat.

Fold reserved liquid into whipped cream.

To serve, pour a little Cranberry Sauce over each fritter, decorate with a tiny Frosted Mint Leaf and add a little whipped cream.

Rich Secret Desserts

Twelve 1¼in (3cm) portions

6 ounces (150g) marzipan
12 thick squares dark dessert chocolate
1 quantity batter from Fruit Fritters recipe using rum in place of water

To serve
4 tablespoons (4 × 15ml spoons) whipped cream
1 tablespoon (1 × 15ml spoon) grated chocolate

Divide marzipan into 12 pieces and roll each piece into a square large enough to wrap round a piece of chocolate. Mould marzipan round chocolate to enclose.

Using tongs, dip the pieces in batter and deep-fry for 2 to 3 minutes until golden brown. Drain on kitchen paper and keep warm.

To serve, swirl a little cream on each plate and place a fritter to one side. Sprinkle a little grated chocolate over each fritter.

Caribbean Tipsies

Twelve 1½in (4cm) fritters

12 fresh dates
2 ounces (50g) creamed coconut
1 quantity batter from Fruit Fritters recipe made with white wine in place of water

Coconut sauce
3 tablespoons (3 × 15ml spoons) flaked coconut
6 tablespoons (6 × 15ml spoons) thickly set yoghurt

Split each date and remove the stones. Cut the creamed coconut into 12 equal pieces and use to stuff the dates. Dip dates in batter and deep-fry for 2 to 3 minutes until golden brown. Drain on kitchen paper and keep warm.

To make the sauce, stir 1 tablespoon (1 × 15ml spoon) flaked coconut into the yoghurt. Serve each fritter with a spoonful of sauce. Sprinkle extra coconut over the fritters and sauce.

Strawberry Fritters

Twelve 1½in (4cm) fritters

12 firm large strawberries
1 quantity batter from Fruit Fritters recipe
2 tablespoons (2 × 15ml spoons) icing sugar

To serve
4 tablespoons (4 × 15ml spoons) whipped cream

Remove hulls from strawberries. Dip strawberries into the batter and deep-fry for 1 minute, then remove from fat and re-dip in batter. Return the fritters to the oil and fry for 2 to 3 minutes until golden brown. Drain on kitchen paper and keep warm.

Sift icing sugar over fritters and serve with whipped cream.

Two into one
You can, if you wish, halve the quantities of fruit and other ingredients in these recipes and use the basic quantity of batter to make two batches (about six portions each) using different fruits.

Meringues, Macaroons

Meringues come in many guises, and can be flavoured with chocolate, coffee and nuts; fillings provide all kinds of complementary tastes. Macaroons are rich almond biscuits.

French Meringue

This simple combination of egg white and sugar can be shaped into shells, and vacherins for combining with exotic ingredients.

French Meringue

About 10 portions

1 egg white
2 ounces (50g) caster sugar or soft brown sugar

Make sure that no egg yolk is present. Place the white in a dry grease-free bowl, preferably copper or a mixer bowl. Whisk slowly at first then on high speed until the foam is stiff. Whisk in half the sugar until the meringue is stiff and shiny. Sprinkle the remaining sugar over and fold in gently with a spatula or metal spoon, cutting through the mixture and turning it over until all the sugar is mixed in.

Shape or pipe on to non-stick baking parchment on a baking sheet. Dry out in a very cool oven or warming drawer, 200°F, 100°C, Gas Mark ¼.

Chocolate
Add 1 ounce (25g) grated plain chocolate with the second half of the sugar.

Hazelnut
Fold 1 ounce (25g) Toasted Chopped Hazelnuts* with the sugar. Shape and dry out the meringue before the oil in the nuts makes the foam collapse.

Almond
Fold in 1 ounce (25g) ground almonds and one drop of almond extract.

Coffee
Mix 1 teaspoon (5ml spoon) instant coffee powder or finely ground filter coffee with the sugar before folding in. The meringue is attractively speckled.

Meringue Discs

Sixteen 2in (5cm) discs

Cut non-stick baking parchment to fit a baking sheet and draw 2in (5cm) circles a little apart. Fit a nylon piping bag with a ¼in (6mm) plain piping tube and fill with French Meringue, flavoured as appropriate. Starting from the centre, pipe meringue in the circles. Bake in a very cool oven 200°F, 100°C, Gas Mark ¼ for about 1 hour until the discs will lift off easily. Cool, then store in an airtight box. Use for the following recipes.

Previous pages, clockwise from left *Apricot and Hazelnut Vacherin (right) surrounded by 1½in (3.5cm) Orange and Walnut Whirls (page 125); Rose Cream Meringues (page 122); Macaroons (page 129) surrounded by Chocolate Mint (page 124) and Mocha Meringues (page 124) and Coconut Macaroons (page 129); Valentine Pavlova (page 128); Walnut Macaroons (page 129); Strawberry Meringue Gâteau (opposite).*

Apricot and Hazelnut Vacherins

Four 2in (5cm) vacherins

1 ounce (25g) dried apricots
2 tablespoon (2 × 15ml spoons) clear honey
2 fluid ounces (50ml) boiling water
2 fluid ounces (50ml) double cream
8 Meringue Discs with hazelnut flavouring (above)
6 pistachio nuts, chopped

Liquidize apricots and honey together with the boiling water; leave 15 minutes.

Whisk the cream until stiff. Whisk in half the apricot purée and use to sandwich the meringues. Top each vacherin with chopped pistachio nuts and serve with the remaining apricot sauce poured over.

Thin the sauce with a little more honey if it is too thick to pour.

Raspberry Tie-Ups

Four 2in (5cm) raspberry tie-ups

A drop of green food colouring
1 ounce (25g) white marzipan
12 raspberries
1 quantity Chantilly Cream filling (page 122)
8 Meringue Discs with almond flavouring
    (opposite)

Knead a drop of colouring into the marzipan, roll out and trim to a 9 × 1in (23 × 2.5cm) strip. Cut into four strips ¼in (6mm) wide.

Crush 8 raspberries and mix into the cream. Sandwich the discs with this cream filling and place a raspberry on top of each.

Cut one strip of marzipan in half and attach underneath a filled vacherin at opposite sides. Tie over the top of the raspberry. Repeat with remaining meringues.

Vacherin Chantilly with Raspberry Sauce

Four 2in (5cm) vacherins

4 ounces (100g) raspberries
1 ounce (50g) caster sugar
1 tablespoon (1 × 15ml spoon) kirsch
8 Meringue Discs with almond flavouring
    (opposite), topped with a sprinkling of flaked
    almonds before baking
1 quantity Chantilly Cream filling (page 122)
1 teaspoon (1 × 5ml spoon) icing sugar, sifted

Cook raspberries gently in a small saucepan until the juice runs. Press through a nylon sieve; mix purée with caster sugar and kirsch. Spread the purée on four small serving plates.

Sandwich the Meringue Discs with Chantilly Cream filling and dredge with icing sugar. Place one in the centre of each plate.

Whisking egg whites
Egg whites will not whisk if there is any grease present. It is best to wash the bowl and beaters in hot soapy water and dry them thoroughly with a clean, dry cloth before starting.

Strawberry Meringue Gâteau

Four to five 4in (10cm) portions

½ quantity French Meringue with hazelnut
    flavouring (opposite)
2 squares chocolate
4 fluid ounces (100ml) double cream
1 tablespoon (1 × 15ml spoon) Grand Marnier
½ teaspoon (1 × 2.5ml spoon) grated orange rind
8 strawberries, sliced
1 tablespoon (1 × 15ml spoon) redcurrant jelly
1 pistachio nut, chopped

Spread or pipe the meringue in two 4in (10cm) marked circles on non-stick baking parchment. Dry out in a cool oven, 200°F, 100°C, Gas Mark ¼, for 1 hour or until circles will lift off the parchment.

Melt the chocolate in a small bowl over hot water and spread over the base of one meringue layer.

Whip the cream until stiff, then whip in the Grand Marnier and orange rind. Spread half over the chocolate meringue base on a serving plate.

Arrange about one-third of the strawberries on the top meringue circle and one-third on the cream. Sandwich together, pipe stars of remaining cream on top and decorate with the chopped pistachio nut. Melt the redcurrant jelly gently and use to glaze the strawberries. Arrange the remaining sliced strawberries on the plate around the gâteau with points outwards. Leave for at least ½ hour for the meringue to soften slightly before serving.

Almond Meringue Towers

Nine 2in (5cm) towers

1 quantity French Meringue with almond
    flavouring (opposite)
1 quantity Chocolate Cream filling (page 122)
1 tablespoon (1 × 15ml spoon) icing sugar, sifted
Pink Marzipan Daisies*

Fit a nylon piping bag with a ¼in (6mm) plain piping tube. Fill with meringue (page 000) and pipe nine 2in (5cm), nine 1½in (3.5cm) and nine small beads on to non-stick baking parchment. Dry out in a cool oven 200°F, 100°C, Gas Mark ¼ for about 1 hour until meringues easily lift off the parchment.

Whisk Chocolate Cream until thick, then pipe with a small star tube to layer the meringues. Leave ½ hour before serving to soften slightly then dredge with icing sugar, and decorate each with 6 tiny pink Marzipan Daisies.

Mini Meringue Shells

Twenty 1in (2.5cm) shells; 10 portions

Cover a baking sheet with non-stick baking parchment. Take a heaped teaspoonful of flavoured French Meringue (page 120), smooth the top to form a dome then use another teaspoon to scoop the meringue on to the parchment. Shape an even number then dry out for about 1 hour until they easily lift off the parchment. Use vanilla, chocolate, coffee or hazelnut flavoured meringue, according to the fillings.

Fillings

2 fluid ounces (50ml) double cream

Chantilly Cream
Whisk the cream with 1 teaspoon (1 × 5ml spoon) caster sugar and a few drops of real vanilla extract.

Chocolate Cream
Break up 1 ounce (25g) dessert plain chocolate, place in a basin and heat in a microwave oven or gently in a small saucepan with the cream. Cool, chill, then add 1 tablespoon (1 × 15ml spoon) dark rum.

Coffee Cream
Dissolve 1 teaspoon (1 × 5ml spoon) instant coffee in 1 teaspoon (1 × 5ml spoon) boiling water. Whisk into the cream.

Praline Cream
Whisk 2 teaspoons (2 × 5ml spoons) Praline* into the cream.

Orange Cream
Whisk 1 teaspoon (1 × 5ml spoon) finely grated orange rind into the cream. Add a tiny drop of orange food colouring, if desired.

Lemon Cream
Whisk 1 teaspoon (1 × 5ml spoon) finely grated lemon rind into the cream.

Liqueur or Brandy Cream
Whisk 1 tablespoon (1 × 15ml spoon) Tia Maria, Grand Marnier, Cointreau, curaçao, crème de menthe or brandy into the cream.

Rose Cream Meringues

Five 2in (5cm) filled meringues

1 quantity Chantilly Cream filling
1 teaspoon (5ml spoon) rose water
10 Mini Meringue Shells, each sprinkled with a
  pinch of Coloured Crystals* before baking
5 Frosted Rose Petals*

Whisk Chantilly Cream filling with rose water. Pipe between 2 shells, arrange on a plate and decorate each with a Frosted Rose Petal.

Meringue Belle Hélène

Five 2in (5cm) filled meringues

2 ounces (50g) plain chocolate, chopped
½ teaspoon (1 × 2.5ml spoon) instant coffee
  powder
3 tablespoons (3 × 15ml spoons) water
1 rounded teaspoon (2 × 5ml spoons) golden syrup
1 small ripe pear
1 tablespoon (1 × 15ml spoon) kirsch
Five 1in (2.5cm) cubes Vanilla Ice Cream (page
  136)
10 Mini Meringue Shells

Place the chocolate, coffee powder, water and golden syrup in a small saucepan. Heat gently until the chocolate has melted, then simmer for 2 minutes.

Peel the pear, cut into five wedges and turn these in the kirsch to prevent browning.

To serve, sandwich a cube of ice cream between 2 Meringue Shells, place a pear wedge on top and pour hot chocolate sauce over.

Quantities
To make ten 1in (2.5cm) flavoured meringue shells, reduce the flavouring ingredients by half and add to half the French Meringue mixture.

Right, clockwise from top left *Orange and Walnut Whirls (page 125); 1in (2.5cm) Meringue Stars (page 125); Orange and Walnut Whirls (page 125).*

Chocolate Chip Meringues

Five 2in (5cm) filled meringues

*10 Mini Meringue Shells (page 122) made with
   chocolate flavoured French Meringue (page 120)*
1 quantity Orange Cream filling (page 122)
1 tablespoon (1 × 15ml spoon) Cointreau
A few drops orange food colouring
Shreds of orange rind, thinly cut

Sandwich the Mini Meringue Shells with Orange
Cream filling, whisked until stiff with Cointreau and
tinted pale orange with food colouring.
   Sprinkle shreds of orange rind over the cream.

Mocha Meringues

Five 2in (5cm) filled meringues

*10 Mini Meringue Shells (page 122) made with
   coffee flavoured French Meringue (page 120)*
1 quantity Chocolate Cream filling (page 122)
5 chocolate coffee bean sweets

Sandwich the Mini Meringue Shells with Chocolate
Cream filling and top each with a chocolate coffee
bean.
   Place in petits fours cases (optional).

Jamaica Meringues

Five 2in (5cm) filled meringues

1 ounce (25g) raisins
3 tablespoons (3 × 15ml spoons) dark rum
1 ounce (25g) sponge cake crumbs
*10 Mini Meringue Shells with coffee flavour (as
   above)*
1 tablespoon (1 × 15ml spoon) icing sugar
5 pineapple pieces, cut very small

Chop raisins finely and soak in the rum for 1 hour.
Mix in the cake crumbs, then sandwich the Mini
Meringue Shells with this filling.
   Dredge them with icing sugar and decorate each
with a tiny piece of pineapple.

Hazelnut Chantilly Meringues

Five 2in (5cm) filled meringues

*10 Mini Meringue Shells (page 122) made with
   hazelnut flavoured French Meringue (page 120)*
1 quantity Chantilly Cream filling (page 122)
2 squares plain chocolate
1 teaspoon (1 × 5ml spoon) honey

Sandwich the Mini Meringue Shells with Chantilly
Cream filling.
   Melt the chocolate in a small basin over hot water
with the honey. Spoon into a cone of greaseproof
paper, snip off the point and pipe zig-zags of
chocolate over the meringues and cream. Leave to
set, then place in petits fours cases.

Marnier Meringues

Five 2in (5cm) filled meringues

*1 quantity Liqueur Cream filling with Grand
   Marnier flavour (page 122)*
*10 Mini Meringue Shells (page 122) made with
   hazelnut flavoured French Meringue (page 120)*
5 mandarin orange segments

After whipping, pipe Liqueur Cream filling between
5 pairs of Mini Meringue Shells. Decorate each
serving with a mandarin orange segment.

Chocolate Mint Meringues

Five 2in (5cm) filled meringues

A few drops green food colouring
*1 quantity Liqueur Cream filling (page 122) with
   crème de menthe*
*10 Mini Meringue Shells (page 122) made with
   chocolate flavoured French Meringue(page 120)*
5 Frosted Mint Leaves*

Whisk the food colouring into the Liqueur Cream
filling to tint pale green. Pipe between pairs of Mini
Meringue Shells and place in paper cases.
   Decorate each with a tiny Frosted Mint Leaf.

Meringue Cuite

This is the easiest meringue to make. It does not need baking, unless it is used for a tall basket and can be flavoured, tinted with food colouring and piped in shapes to form the base for desserts.

Meringue Cuite

1 egg white
3 ounces (75g) icing sugar

Place the egg white and icing sugar in a small, very clean basin. Place basin over a small saucepan of boiling water and remove from the heat. Whisk on high speed, with an electric whisk if possible, until the meringue is very stiff and stands in peaks.

Colour and flavour as in the following recipes, then pipe or shape on to non-stick baking parchment. Leave in a warm dry place overnight to dry out.

Meringue Stars

Use these for topping trifles and decorating desserts. Sandwich together with Chocolate Cream (page 122) or Rich Butter Cream*.

Eighteen 1in (2.5cm) meringue stars

1 quantity Meringue Cuite
A drop each of yellow, green, pink and mauve food
  colourings

Divide the stiffly whisked meringue into five cups. Add a drop of food colouring to each one, leaving one white.

Fit a nylon piping bag with a star tube and pipe stars of meringue on to non-stick baking parchment. Start with white, then fill bag with yellow then green meringue to avoid washing the bag and tube. Wash and dry the bag and tube before filling with pink then mauve meringue.

Dry out overnight in a warm dry place then lift off the parchment and store in an airtight tin or plastic box.

Orange and Walnut Whirls

Makes six 1½in (3.5cm) whirls

½ quantity Meringue Cuite
1 teaspoon (1 × 5ml spoon) finely grated orange
  rind
1 drop orange food colouring
6 walnut halves

Bases

1 ounce (25g) butter
1 ounce (25g) icing sugar
½ teaspoon (1 × 2.5ml spoon) instant coffee
1 teaspoon (1 × 5ml spoon) boiling water
1 ounce (25g) digestive biscuits
1 ounce (25g) chopped walnuts
2 ounces (50g) cream cheese
1 teaspoon (1 × 5ml spoon) grated orange rind
1 teaspoon (1 × 5ml spoon) orange juice
1 teaspoon (1 × 5ml spoon) icing sugar

Whisk meringue with orange rind and colouring and pipe six 1½in (3.5cm) whirls on to non-stick baking parchment. Place a walnut half on each and leave overnight to dry out.

Cream butter and icing sugar in a small bowl until soft and fluffy. Dissolve instant coffee in boiling water and add to butter mixture. Crush biscuits and add to the bowl with the walnuts. Form into six balls then flatten with a knife.

Beat cream cheese with orange rind, juice and icing sugar. Divide between the bases and place a meringue on each.

Keeping meringues
Though meringues will freeze successfully, they need protecting in sturdy boxes. It is easier to store them just in the cupboard as they have a long life when unfilled.

Pavlova

This meringue with a soft centre, a native of Australia and New Zealand, is often preferred to the crisper French type. It can be used in most of the same ways. Because it is cooked at a slightly higher temperature than French meringue, Pavlova is more creamy coloured. It stores well and will keep in an airtight tin or plastic box for up to two weeks. Pavlova needs to be whisked very stiffly, preferably with an electric whisk.

Australian Pavlova

For 10 to 12 portions

1 large (size 1) egg white
3 ounces (75g) caster sugar
½ teaspoon (1 × 2.5ml spoon) vinegar
½ teaspoon (1 × 2.5ml spoon) vanilla extract
½ teaspoon (1 × 2.5ml spoon) cornflour

Prepare a cool oven at 300°F, 150°C, Gas Mark 2. Line a baking sheet with non-stick baking parchment.

Whisk egg white until stiff; gradually whisk in all of the sugar at top speed. Blend vinegar, vanilla extract and cornflour together in a small bowl and whisk into the meringue. The meringue should be very stiff and glossy. Shape or pipe on to the baking parchment.

Reduce oven heat to very cool at 250°F, 120°C, Gas Mark ½, and bake pavlova for the time given in each recipe. Leave to cool in the oven.

Passion Fruit Pavlovas

Five 2in (5cm) pavlovas

½ quantity Australian Pavlova mixture
5 tablespoons (5 × 15ml spoons) Diplomat Cream*
1 passion fruit
15 pink Marzipan Hearts* for decoration

Prepare a cool oven at 300°F, 150°C, Gas Mark 2.

Draw five 2in (5cm) circles on non-stick baking parchment and pipe meringue in the circles. Pipe a wall of stars around each. Place in the oven, turn down the heat to very cool at 250°F, 120°C, Gas Mark ½ and leave for 40 minutes. Turn off the oven and allow pavlovas to cool in oven.

To serve, place Diplomat Cream in a small basin. Cut the passion fruit in half and add fruit to the basin; mix well then divide between the pavlovas. Decorate with tiny pink Marzipan Hearts.

Coffee Meringue Fingers

Six × 2½in (6.5cm) fingers

2 teaspoons (2 × 5ml spoons) instant coffee
½ teaspoon (1 × 2.5ml spoon) water
½ quantity Australian Pavlova mixture
Finely chopped walnuts
¼ quantity Rich Butter Cream* flavoured with 2 teaspoons (2 × 5ml spoons) Tia Maria
2 ounces (50g) plain chocolate

Heat oven to 300°F, 150°C, Gas Mark 2.

Dissolve coffee in the water and whisk into the pavlova mixture. Fit a nylon piping bag with a ½in (1.25cm) star piping tube, fill with pavlova mixture and pipe 2½in (6.5cm) bars in a zig-zag action like a corkscrew on non-stick baking parchment. Sprinkle with finely chopped walnuts and place in the oven. Reduce heat immediately to very cool (250°F, 120°C, Gas Mark ½) and leave to dry out for ½ hour. Turn off the heat and leave pavlova in the oven until cold.

Sandwich pavlova fingers in pairs with Rich Butter Cream. Melt chocolate in a small basin over hot water and dip the ends of the meringues in the chocolate. Leave to set on non-stick baking parchment, then store in a tin.

Right, from top Raspberry Tie-Up (page 121); 2in (5cm) Almond Meringue Towers (page 121); Apricot and Hazelnut Vacherin (page 120).

Valentine Pavlovas

Five 3in (7.5cm) pavlovas

½ quantity Australian Pavlova mixture (page 126)
2 tablespoons (2 × 15ml spoons) Praline*

Filling
½lb (200g) raspberries
1 teaspoon (1 × 5ml spoon) caster sugar
2 fluid ounces (50ml) double cream
10 tiny Frosted Flowers*

Draw five heart shapes 3in (7.5cm) long on non-stick baking parchment. Heat oven to 300°F, 150°C, Gas Mark 2.

Make up the pavlova mixture as directed and fold in the Praline when stiff. Work quickly as the Praline will soften the foam. Fit a nylon piping bag with a medium-sized star tube and fill with 3 heaped tablespoons (15ml spoons) of the mixture. Spread remaining mixture in the heart shapes, then pipe shells around. Place in the oven, turn down the heat to very cool at 250°F, 120°C, Gas Mark ½ and leave for 40 minutes. Turn off the oven and allow the pavlovas to cool.

Cook raspberries until the juice is released. Press through a nylon sieve to make a purée; add sugar, then cool. Whisk cream until stiff, gradually whisk in the purée, then spread in each pavlova. Decorate each dessert with Frosted Flowers.

Apricot Pavlovas

Six 2½in (6cm) pavlovas

2 fluid ounces (50ml) double cream
2 teaspoons (2 × 5ml spoons) Amaretto liqueur
6 round Australian Pavlovas (page 126) with piped
    sides
3 fresh apricots or 6 canned apricot halves
1 tablespoon (1 × 15ml spoon) Apricot Glaze*

Whip the cream with the liqueur and place a teaspoonful (5ml spoon) in each pavlova.

If fresh apricots are used, cut in halves and poach for 4 minutes in sugar syrup in a saucepan. Drain, dry on kitchen paper and cool. Place one half in each pavlova. Brush with warmed Apricot Glaze.

Citrus Meringue Bar

One 5 × 3in (12.5 × 7.5cm) bar; 4−5 slices

½ quantity Australian Pavlova mixture (page 126)

Filling
1 egg yolk
1 ounce (25g) caster sugar
Finely grated rind and juice of ½ lemon
1 fluid ounce (25ml) double cream
5 mandarin orange segments
5 black grapes
6 Marzipan Leaves*

Prepare a cool oven at 300°F, 150°C, Gas Mark 2. Draw two oblongs, each 5 × 3in (12.5 × 7.5cm) on non-stick baking parchment.

Place the meringue in a piping bag fitted with a large star tube and pipe about three-quarters of the meringue into each oblong. Pipe shells around the edge of one to form a case. Place meringue in the oven and immediately reduce temperature to very cool at 250°F, 120°C, Gas Mark ½. Leave to dry out for 35 minutes then turn the oven off and leave until oven is cold.

To make the filling, whisk egg yolk, sugar, rind and juice of 1 lemon in a small basin over a saucepan of boiling water until the mixture is thick and leaves a trail when the whisk is lifted. Remove basin from the heat and whisk the mixture until cool. In another small bowl whisk the cream until thick then fold into the lemon mixture.

Spread half the filling on each pavlova layer. Arrange mandarin orange segments over top layer; cut the grapes in half, remove the pips and arrange with the oranges. Sandwich the layers together. Decorate with Marzipan Leaves. Assemble at least 1 hour before serving to make the dessert easy to cut. Cut into five slices.

Ingredients, sauces, edible containers, etc that are asterisked in the recipes on these pages are given in detail on pages 147 to 156. For exact page numbers, refer to the index at the end of the book.

Macaroons

Macaroons are sweet confections of minced or ground nuts. Almonds are traditional, but walnuts, hazelnuts and coconut all make delicious sweet, chewy biscuits. In Italy, a proportion of bitter almonds is added, while Austrian macaroons often contain hazelnuts, walnuts or chocolate. Rice flour is sometimes included to improve the texture. Macaroons are usually piped on to rice paper and decorated with a split almond or a glacé cherry. When the mixture is used for gâteaux, it is best to pipe it on to non-stick baking parchment.

Macaroons

About thirty-six 1in (2.5cm) macaroons

4 ounces (100g) caster sugar
2 ounces (50g) ground almonds
1 teaspoon (1 × 5ml spoon) ground rice
1 large egg white
1 drop almond extract
Sheet of rice paper
About 36 split almonds

Mix sugar, almonds and rice in a medium bowl. Add egg white and almond extract and beat with a wooden spoon or electric whisk until the mixture is thick. Leave for 15 minutes.

Place a sheet of rice paper on a baking sheet, shiny side down. Prepare a moderate oven (350°F, 180°C, Gas Mark 4).

Beat the macaroon mixture again until very thick and white, then place in a nylon piping bag fitted with a ½in (1.25cm) plain tube. Pipe in 1in (2.5cm) rounds (or as directed in the recipes that follow), leaving room for them to spread. Place a split almond in the centre of each. Bake for about 20 minutes until set and pale golden brown.

Fingers

Pipe the macaroon mixture in 2in (5cm) lengths, using a nylon piping bag fitted with a ½in (1.25cm) plain tube.

Storage of macaroons
Store macaroons in tins or airtight plastic boxes. They will keep for up to 4 weeks. The macaroons will soften slightly but the taste will develop.

Hazelnut Macaroons

Toast 2 ounces (50g) hazelnuts under a moderate grill or in a hot oven until browned. Cool, then slip off the skins and grind the hazelnuts finely in a liquidizer or food processor, or chop them very finely.

Follow the recipe for Almond Macaroons, but replace the ground almonds with these hazelnuts, adding 1 drop of vanilla extract instead of the almond extract. Place a hazelnut in the centre of each macaroon.

Walnut Macaroons
Replace hazelnuts with untoasted, chopped walnuts.

Coconut Macaroons

Follow the recipe for Almond Macaroons, but replace the ground almonds with desiccated coconut and omit the almond extract. Top with pieces of glacé cherry.

Hazelnut Macaroon Deckers

Three 2in (5cm) deckers

Six 2in (5cm) Hazelnut Macaroons (without whole nuts on top)
Three 2in (5cm) Meringue Discs (page 120)
1 quantity Liqueur Cream filling (page 122), flavoured with orange curaçao
Meringue Stars (page 125) flavoured with ½ teaspoon (1 × 5ml spoon) finely grated orange rind

Layer a Hazelnut Macaroon, a French Meringue, then another Hazelnut Macaroon with Liqueur Cream. Leave to soften for ½ hour before serving, and decorate each with a star.

Iced Desserts

Iced desserts include simple ice creams, spectacular gâteaux and bombes, tangy water ices, granitas and smooth sorbets. They can all be made in a freezer, or the ice-making compartment of a refrigerator.

Ice Creams

These include smooth, creamy ices made from a mixture of rich cream and fruit purée, moscovites, which have a softly set, mousse-like texture, and classic custard-based ice creams flavoured and shaped to make all kinds of desserts.

Fruit Purée Ice Cream

This recipe is suitable for raspberries, strawberries, gooseberries, cranberries, mulberries, blackcurrants, redcurrants, peaches, apricots, nectarines, mangosteen, melon, chestnut, apples, pears, oranges, lemons, limes, bananas and cherries. Fresh or canned fruit may be used.

1 pint (400ml); 8 portions

½ lb (200g) fruit
Caster sugar to taste
1 egg, separated
2 ounces (50g) icing sugar
8 fluid ounces (200ml) double cream

Prepare the fruit: liquidize and sieve raw berry fruit, apricots, peaches and nectarines, or cook the harder fruits in a little water or wine before liquidizing, sieving and chilling. Add caster sugar to taste.

Whisk the egg white until it forms soft peaks. Gradually whisk in the icing sugar then the egg yolk. Fold in the fruit purée and pour the mixture into a large freezer container. Freeze for 1 hour or until the ice cream is firm 1in (2.5cm) around the edge. Quickly beat the mixture with an electric whisk until it is smooth, or turn it into a chilled food processor bowl and process until smooth. Whisk the cream until it forms soft peaks. Fold into the half-set ice cream and return it to the freezer. Freeze for 1 hour then repeat the beating. Cover with foil and freeze until firm.

Before serving, place in the refrigerator for about 45 minutes to soften slightly.

Apple and Ginger Ice Cream

1 pint (400ml); 6 to 8 portions

½ lb (250g) prepared cooking apples
2 tablespoons (2 × 15ml spoons) syrup from jar of stem ginger
Knob of butter
1 quantity Fruit Purée Ice Cream (using the apples to make the purée)
2 pieces stem ginger
6 teaspoons (6 × 5ml spoons) ginger syrup

Peel, core and slice the apples. Simmer with ginger syrup and butter until soft. Beat until smooth. Cool, then chill.

Proceed as basic recipe.

Finely chop ginger and stir in after final beating.

To serve, scoop into small glasses and spoon a little ginger syrup over each portion.

Red Cherry Ice Cream

1 pint (400ml); 8 portions

14.4 ounce (410g) can of red cherries
2 tablespoons (2 × 15ml spoons) maraschino de cuisine
1 quantity Fruit Purée Ice Cream (using cherries for purée)

Remove any stones from the cherries. Liquidize, sieve, stir in the liqueur and chill. Proceed as basic recipe.

Previous pages, from left *Single scoops of ice cream: Pina Colada Ice Cream (page 136); Raspberry Moscovite (page 134); Chocolate Chip and Raisin (page 137); Gooseberry and Walnut Ice Cream (opposite); Blue Cheese Moscovite (page 134).*

Gooseberry and Walnut Ice Cream

1 pint (400ml); 8 portions

½ lb (200g) gooseberries
1 head elderflower (optional)
Juice of ½ orange
1 quantity Fruit Purée Ice Cream (using
  gooseberries for purée)
Green food colouring
1 ounce (25g) shelled walnuts

To serve
Chopped walnuts

Simmer gooseberries with elderflower (if used) and orange juice until soft. Sieve gooseberries, cool, then chill the purée.

Proceed as basic recipe tinting ice cream with food colouring as required.

Chop walnuts finely and fold in after final beating.

Sprinkle each portion with chopped walnuts before serving.

Chestnut and Rum Ice Cream

1 pint (400ml); 8 portions

4 tablespoons (4 × 15ml spoons) sweetened
  chestnut purée
1 fluid ounce (25ml) dark rum
1 quantity Fruit Purée Ice Cream, omitting egg yolk
  and using only half the icing sugar

To serve
8 Chocolate Cases*
Pieces of marron glacé

Beat chestnut purée with the rum. Fold the meringue mixture into the purée. Proceed as basic recipe.

Cube and serve in Chocolate Cases, decorated with pieces of marron glacé.

Red Berry Yoghurt Ice Cream

1 pint (400ml); 8 portions

½ lb (250g) raspberries, strawberries, loganberries
  or mulberries
1 quantity Fruit Purée Ice Cream, with 8 fluid
  ounces (200ml) thickly set natural yoghurt
  instead of cream

Follow basic recipe, using the red berries to make the purée, but reserving 8 berries for decoration.

Substitute yoghurt for the cream and gently fold in. Proceed as basic recipe.

Serve small scoops in sherry glasses and top each portion with a berry.

Soft-Set Moscovite

Suitable for soft fruits, plums, damsons, greengages, red- and blackcurrants, peaches, nectarines, apricots, melon, cherries, citrus fruits, kiwi fruit and mango.

1¼ pints (500ml); 10 portions

2 teaspoons (2 × 5ml spoons) gelatine
½ pint (250ml) fruit purée
2 egg whites
2 ounces (75g) caster sugar
½ pint (250ml) single cream

Place gelatine with 2 tablespoons (2 × 15ml spoons) warm water in a small basin. Place basin over a pan of hot water until gelatine has melted. Cool. Stir into fruit purée. Place the purée in the refrigerator and chill for 15 minutes until softly set. Beat mixture.

Whisk egg whites until they form soft peaks, then whisk in the sugar and fold meringue into the purée. Stir in the cream. Place mixture in a freezer container. Cover and freeze at least 2 hours. No beating is required.

Place moscovites in the refrigerator for about ½ hour before serving, to soften slightly.

Moscovites
These are a cross between a fruit ice and a sorbet. Not as rich as ice creams, or as stiffly frozen as sorbets, they need gelatine in order to set.

Raspberry Moscovite

1¼ pints (500ml); 10 portions

1 quantity Soft-Set Moscovite recipe (page 133)
*   using ½ pint (250ml) raspberry purée, sieved*
6 tablespoons (6 × 15ml spoons) Framboise Eau de
*   Vie liqueur*
4 ounces (100g) raspberries

To serve
Raspberry Sauce*
10 raspberries

Follow basic recipe, stirring the liqueur in with the purée.

Chop the raspberries and fold in just before placing the ice cream in the freezer container.

Serve with Raspberry Sauce, topped with a raspberry.

Peach or Apricot Moscovite

About 1¼ pints (500ml); 10 portions

1 quantity Soft-Set Moscovite recipe (page 133)
*   using ½ pint (250ml) peach or apricot purée*
4 tablespoons (4 × 15ml spoons) apricot brandy

Decoration
Toasted Flaked Almonds*

Make as for basic recipe, stirring the apricot brandy in with the purée.

Serve in tiny scoops or cubes in sherry glasses. Decorate with the Toasted Flaked Almonds.

Banana and Rum Moscovite

About 1¼ pints (500ml); 10 portions

1 quantity Soft-Set Moscovite recipe (page 133)
*   replacing fruit purée with 4 large ripe bananas*
2 tablespoons (2 × 15ml spoons) caster sugar
6 tablespoons (6 × 15ml spoons) white rum
2 tablespoons (2 × 15ml spoons) lemon juice

To serve
10 Chocolate Cases*

Mash the bananas with the sugar, while the melted gelatine is cooling, and mix them with the rum and lemon juice. Stir gelatine quickly into bananas, then continue with basic recipe.

Serve in tiny scoops in Chocolate Cases.

Blue Cheese Moscovite

Eight 1in (2.5cm) cubes

8 ounces (200g) medium-fat soft curd cheese
2 tablespoons (2 × 15ml spoons) orange juice
Grated rind of ½ an orange
½ quantity Soft-Set Moscovite recipe (page 133),
*   without purée. Replace the single cream with*
*   ½ pint (250ml) thick-set natural yoghurt.*
2 ounces (50g) blue-veined Stilton cheese

To serve
Coupelles (page 65)

Beat the curd cheese until smooth; add orange juice and orange rind. Stir into basic recipe instead of the purée.

Roughly chop the Stilton and fold it into the mixture just before placing in a shallow freezer container.

Serve in small chilled dishes with Coupelles.

Ginger and Yoghurt Moscovite

¾ pint (375ml); 5 portions

½ quantity Soft-Set Moscovite recipe (page 133)
*   replacing the cream with ¼ pint (125ml) thick-set*
*   natural yoghurt*
¼ pint (125ml) apple purée
2 pieces stem ginger
2 ginger biscuits, finely crushed

Decoration
Crushed ginger biscuits

Make basic recipe using apple purée and stirring in yoghurt instead of the cream. Finely chop the ginger and fold in with the crushed biscuits just before placing the mixture in a freezer container.

Scoop the Moscovite into small, chilled glasses and sprinkle the remaining crushed ginger biscuits on top. Serve immediately.

Right, from left *Granita de Menthe (page 141) served in a sherry glass; Lemon Water Ice (page 141); Blackcurrant Sorbet with Champagne (page 140).*

Vanilla Ice Cream

1 pint (400ml); 8 portions

1 vanilla pod
³⁄₄ pint (375ml) single cream
3 egg yolks
3 ounces (75g) caster sugar
¹⁄₂ pint (250ml) double cream

Place the vanilla pod and single cream in a heavy-based saucepan and heat slowly to just below boiling point. Remove from the heat and leave to cool. Remove the vanilla pod and re-heat the cream to simmering point.

Place egg yolks and sugar in a bowl and beat until pale and creamy. Stir in the single cream. Return mixture to the saucepan and stir over a low heat until the mixture thickens and coats the back of the spoon. Do not boil or the mixture will separate. Pour custard into a large bowl and stir occasionally until cool.

Whisk the double cream until it forms soft peaks. Fold into the custard mixture and place in a large freezer container. Chill, then place in freezer and leave for 1 hour. Remove and beat the mixture with a whisk, or in the chilled bowl of a food processor until smooth. Repeat after a further hour. Stir in the flavouring. Cover and freeze a further 2 hours or more.

Put in the refrigerator for about 45 minutes to soften slightly before serving.

Almond Ice Cream

³⁄₄ pint (375ml); 6 portions

1 ounce (25g) ratafias
1in (2.5cm) piece angelica
¹⁄₂ quantity Vanilla Ice Cream recipe
1 fluid ounce (25ml) Amaretto liqueur

To serve
Hot Chocolate Sauce*

Roughly chop ratafias. Finely chop angelica and fold into the ice cream after the final beating with the ratafias and Amaretto. Finish as for basic recipe. Serve in sherry glasses with Hot Chocolate Sauce.

Chocolate Ice Cream

³⁄₄ pint (375ml); 6 portions

¹⁄₂ quantity Vanilla Ice Cream recipe
4 ounces (100g) dessert chocolate
2 tablespoons (2 × 15ml spoons) milk

To serve
6 teaspoons (6 × 5ml spoons) orange, mint or coffee liqueur

Follow the basic recipe until the custard thickens and remove from heat. Finely chop the chocolate and stir in to hot custard until melted. Stir in the milk. Finish as basic recipe.

Serve tiny scoops in small glasses and top each portion with a teaspoon (5ml spoon) liqueur.

Pina Colada Ice Cream

1 pint (400ml); 8 portions

¹⁄₂ quantity Vanilla Ice Cream recipe
2 ounces (50g) coconut cream
2 ounces (50g) pineapple
2 tablespoons (2 × 15ml spoons) Malibu liqueur

To serve
16 Langues des Chats (page 64)
8 maraschino cherries with stalks

Finely chop coconut cream and place with the cream from the basic recipe in a saucepan. Follow Vanilla Ice Cream recipe until the final beating. Finely chop pineapple. Fold into ice cream with the Malibu liqueur.

Serve with Langues des Chats, and top each portion with a cherry.

Cassata Ice Cream

³⁄₄ pint (375ml); 6 portions

2 ounces (50g) glacé cherries
1 ounce (25g) crystallized ginger
¹⁄₂ quantity Vanilla Ice Cream recipe
2 tablespoons (2 × 15ml spoons) chopped pistachio nuts
2 tablespoons (2 × 15ml spoons) Maraschino liqueur

To serve
6 Chocolate Cases*

Finely chop the cherries and ginger and fold into the ice cream with the nuts and liqueur after the final beating. Finish as for the basic recipe.

Serve in Chocolate Cases.

Brown Bread Ice Cream

¾ pint (375ml); 6 portions

½ quantity Vanilla Ice Cream recipe, using chilled
    evaporated milk instead of cream
2 ounces (50g) butter
1 ounce (25g) caster sugar
2 ounces (50g) fresh brown breadcrumbs
1 fluid ounce (25ml) Tia Maria

Decoration
6 Chocolate Butterflies*

Add whisked evaporated milk to the ice cream
instead of cream. Melt butter and sugar in a
saucepan. Add breadcrumbs and stir over medium
heat until the breadcrumbs are crisp and golden.
Drain, cool and chill.

Beat the breadcrumbs and Tia Maria into the ice
cream with final beating.

Serve in liqueur glasses, and decorate each
portion with a Chocolate Butterfly.

Chocolate Chip and Raisin

¾ pint (375ml); 6 portions

1 ounce (25g) raisins
1 fluid ounce (25ml) dark rum
2 ounces (50g) dessert chocolate
½ quantity Vanilla Ice Cream recipe
6 Duet biscuits (page 69)

Place raisins and rum in a small basin and leave
several hours to macerate.

Finely chop the chocolate and fold into the ice
cream with the raisins after the final beating.

Finish as for basic recipe.

Serve tiny scoops in glasses, with Duet biscuits.

To freeze successfully
For best results, freeze ice creams in a
shallow, metal container.

Iced Gâteaux

Differently flavoured and textured ice creams and sorbets can be combined to
create exotic desserts, mixed and matched in a variety of shapes.

Cassata Roll

One 4½in (11.25cm) roll, 3in (7.5cm) in
diameter; 8 portions

1 quantity Cassata Ice Cream (opposite)
6 ounces (150g) marzipan
A few drops green food colouring

Decoration
2 tablespoons (2 × 15ml spoons) whipped
    cream
A few walnut halves

Place Cassata Ice Cream in a ¾ pint (375ml) empty
food can. Freeze. Unmould the ice cream by
opening the other end of the can and holding it in
your hands for a few minutes before pushing out.

Knead the marzipan with a little food colouring
until evenly coloured. Roll out and trim to 4½ ×
11in (11.5 × 28cm). Place roll on the marzipan and
roll up, putting join underneath. Wrap in cling film.
Place in the freezer until required.

Pipe cream along the top and decorate with
walnut halves. Slice the roll and serve.

Iced Layered Gâteau

One 6 × 3in (15 × 7.5cm) gâteau; 6 portions

½ quantity Vanilla Ice Cream recipe (page 136)
4 ounces (100g) dark dessert chocolate, grated
1 fluid ounce (25ml) dark rum
2 teaspoons (2 × 5ml spoons) instant coffee
*   granules*
One 6 × 3in (15 × 7cm) thin Chocolate
*   Oblong**
Sixteen 1½in (4cm) thin Chocolate
*   Triangles**
Knob of butter
¼ pint (125ml) whipping cream

Follow the basic recipe for Vanilla Ice Cream up to the stage where the custard thickens. Divide the hot custard mixture between two bowls. Stir 4 ounces (100g) chocolate into one and when melted beat in the rum. Stir the coffee granules into the other bowl.

Leave both custards to cool, stirring occasionally. Cover and chill.

Whip the cream from the basic recipe until it forms soft peaks, divide between the bowls and fold in. Place bowls in the freezer for 1 hour, beating twice.

Line two tins or containers, each with a 6 × 3in (15 × 7cm) base, with a strip of foil measuring about 12 × 3in (30 × 7.5cm). After the final beating, pour the ice cream into separate tins, reserve 1 tablespoon (1 × 15ml spoon) of chocolate ice cream for decoration, and return to the freezer for 1 hour.

To Assemble Gâteau

Place Chocolate Oblong on a freezer-proof plate or board. Turn out coffee ice cream and place on top. Repeat with chocolate ice cream. Return to freezer.

Whip cream until stiff, spread over the top and around the sides. Streak in the reserved chocolate ice cream over the top. Decorate the sides with Chocolate Triangles and return the gâteau to the freezer.

Place gâteau in the refrigerator for 30 minutes to soften slightly before serving.

Iced Bombe

Two ¾ pint (375ml) bombes; 12 portions

½ quantity Vanilla Ice Cream (page 136)
1 fluid ounce (25ml) brandy
A few drops yellow food colouring
½ quantity Red Cherry Ice Cream (page 132)

Decoration
3 tablespoons (3 × 15ml spoons) whipped
*   cream*

Place two ¾ pint (375ml) metal moulds in the freezer. Soften the Vanilla Ice Cream and beat in the brandy and a few drops of food colouring to tint yellow. Return ice cream to the freezer until firm but not hard.

Using two-thirds of the Vanilla Ice Cream, spread it thickly round the inside of each mould leaving a suitable space in the centre for filling. Return the moulds to the freezer.

Part freeze the Red Cherry Ice Cream and pack into the centres of the moulds. Level the top and re-freeze.

Spread the reserved Vanilla Ice Cream across the base of each bombe. Cover with foil and return to the freezer until ready to use.

Unmould the bombe by wrapping a cloth, wrung out in hot water, round the mould for a few seconds. Tap mould firmly to release the bombe. Place bombe on a chilled serving plate and put in the refrigerator.

Place cream in a piping bag fitted with a small star tube and use to decorate the bombe. Place in the refrigerator up to 10 minutes before serving or replace in the freezer.

Ingredients, sauces, edible containers, etc that are asterisked in the recipes on these pages are given in detail on pages 147 to 156. For exact page numbers, refer to the index at the end of the book.

Right, from top *Cassata Roll (page 137); 6 × 3in (15 × 7.5cm) Iced Layered Gâteau (this page); Iced Bombe (this page).*

Water Ices, Granitas, Sorbets

Make water ices from juicy citrus fruits and wines and liqueurs to give them a tangy taste. Granitas are perfect for hot days; their tiny crystals are especially refreshing. Serve in tiny chilled glasses, on their own or with fruit purée, liqueur or champagne poured over. Sorbets are strongly flavoured ices made from meringue and fruit purée, and are easy to make because they do not need to be whisked during freezing.

Water Ice

This recipe is suitable for citrus and other juicy fruits, wines and liqueurs.

1 pint (400ml); 8 portions

½ pint (250ml) water
4 ounces (100g) caster sugar
Flavouring (see following recipes)
1 egg white

Place water and sugar in a heavy-based saucepan. Heat gently until the sugar has dissolved, then increase heat and boil rapidly for 2 minutes.

Remove syrup from heat, pour into a basin and stir occasionally until cool. Add flavouring, chill for ½ hour, pour into a large metal bowl, cover with foil and freeze for about 1 hour until the mixture is frozen ½ inch (1.25cm) in from the sides. Remove from the freezer and whisk until mushy or quickly mix in a food processor.

Whisk egg whites until they form soft peaks. Fold into the iced mixture and return to the freezer for 3 hours, stirring at hourly intervals. Cover and freeze until firm. Place water ice in the refrigerator for 30 minutes before serving.

Passion Fruit Water Ice

¾ pint (375ml); 6 portions

½ quantity Water Ice recipe
3 passion fruits

Decoration
*6 Chocolate Hearts**

Halve the passion fruits, scoop out the flesh into a sieve placed over a measuring jug. Stir flesh and leave to drain for 15 minutes, stirring occasionally until only seeds remain in the sieve. Make the juice up to ¼ pint (175ml) with water. Stir into the cooled syrup. Finish as in the basic Water Ice recipe.

Decorate each portion with a Chocolate Heart.

Fruit Sorbets

Suitable fruits are raspberries, strawberries, loganberries, gooseberries, blackberries, apples, pears, peaches, nectarines, apricots, blackcurrants, redcurrants, damsons, plums, greengages, melon, mango, mangosteen, kiwi fruit and mixtures of these fruits.

1 pint (400ml); 8 portions

½ lb (200g) prepared fruit
4 ounces (100g) granulated sugar
2 egg whites
4 ounces (100g) caster sugar

Cook the fruit, if necessary, adding water or wine to moisten, but keeping the fruit concentrated, and sieve if desired.

Add granulated sugar to the fruit and leave to cool, then chill well.

Whisk the egg whites until stiff; gradually whisk in the caster sugar, then the purée, a little at a time. Place in a shallow freezer container, cover with foil and freeze.

Place in the refrigerator for 15 minutes before serving.

Scoop out the sorbet from the container and place in small chilled dishes or serve in wine glasses topped up with champagne.

Successful sorbets
It is important to chill the fruit purée mixture before whisking in the egg white and sugar, and to freeze the sorbet in a shallow container. This will help the mixture freeze smoothly.

Lemon Water Ice

¾ pint (375ml); 6 portions

½ quantity Water Ice recipe
3 small lemons
A little white wine or water (if necessary)

Decoration
Strips of lemon peel

Grate the rinds of 2 lemons and add to the sugar syrup before boiling.

Squeeze the juice from all of the lemons, measure and make up to ¼ pint (125ml) with wine or water (if necessary). Add to the syrup, strain, cool, chill and then part-freeze as described, and continue with the basic recipe.

Decorate each portion with a twist of lemon peel.

Granita de Menthe

¾ pint (375ml); 6 portions

½ quantity Water Ice recipe,
* omitting egg white*
Juice of 1 lime
A little under ¼ pint (125ml) white wine

To serve
6 tablespoons (6 × 15ml spoons) crème de menthe

Make syrup as in basic Water Ice recipe. Measure lime juice and make up to ¼ pint (125ml) with the wine. Stir into the cooled syrup and place in a large-based metal freezer container. Freeze until just beginning to set on the base and round the edge. Stir with a metal spoon and shave the ice to form granules. Re-freeze and repeat until the consistency is like crushed ice or coffee sugar.

Scrape off the granules into chilled small long-stemmed glasses. Pour 1 tablespoon (1 × 15ml spoon) crème de menthe over each portion.

Orange Water Ice

¾ pint (375ml); 6 portions

½ quantity Water Ice recipe
2 large oranges
A little white wine or water (if necessary)

To serve
6 tiny lime or pineapple wedges

Make as for Lemon Water Ice, boiling the grated rind of 1 orange with the sugar syrup.

Serve with lime or pineapple wedges.

Coffee Liqueur Granita

1 pint (400ml); 10 portions

½ quantity Water Ice recipe, omitting egg white and
* replacing the sugar with demerara sugar*
½ pint (250ml) strong freshly filtered black coffee
2 tablespoons (2 × 15ml spoons) chocolate liqueur
* or Tia Maria*

To serve
¼ pint (125ml) whipped cream or Bailey's Irish
* Cream Liqueur*
10 chocolate coffee bean sweets

Make the basic syrup from the Water Ice recipe using demerara sugar instead of granulated. Add the coffee and leave to cool. Part-freeze, then stir in the liqueur.

Repeat freezing and stirring as for Granita de Menthe until the ice granules resemble coffee sugar. Cover and freeze until required.

To serve, scrape off the granules and place in small chilled glasses.

Serve each with a little whipped cream topped with a chocolate coffee bean, or with liqueur poured over.

Gifts

A selection of tiny, delicious desserts is the perfect present on any occasion. One of the pleasures of creating individual recipes is the chance to match the gift to the recipient, and of course to the reason – and the season.

What to Make

For a chocolate-loving friend's winter birthday, put together an assortment of white Chocolate Cases holding Chantilly Cream, topped by miniature red marzipan berries. An over-worked mother with a job and three children would surely appreciate an icing message piped on a row of biscuits, promising a treat a month throughout the year. A summer wedding provides the opportunity for decorative 'bouquets' of tiny pink cakes as centrepieces for every table, each plate wreathed with real flowers.

Here are a few more hints on choosing just the right kinds of desserts and presenting them as imaginatively as possible.

Unless you are sure that your present will be used immediately, choose recipes that will stay fresh, or can easily be refrigerated or, even better, frozen. The desserts can then be enjoyed over weeks rather than days. Butter cream will be better than fresh cream for fillings; pieces of candied or preserved fruit make long-lasting decorations, more suitable in the circumstances than fresh fruit.

Pastries and biscuits are probably safer to transport than jellies or creams. However, it is possible to give even moulded desserts – with the right kind of protective packaging. Individual portions can sometimes be refrigerated or frozen, ready to serve up to three months later.

Presentation

Presentation is one of the most important aspects of making gifts. The wrappings should reflect the occasion, complement the desserts and make it easy to carry the present safely without upsetting the contents.

Make a habit – which can become a fruitful hobby – of collecting small containers. Look for wide-necked jars which can hold fragile decorations like Frosted Flowers and Chocolate Shapes; you won't necessarily need the lids because you can use cling film under covers specially made from gift paper or fabric.

Glass, either clear or coloured, always looks wonderful – make sure it is scrupulously clean and sparkling before you put anything inside. Fill some pretty, tall, narrow vases with layers of Frosted Petals in a variety of colours, or tiny Meringue Stars and silver balls.

Antique stalls and junk shops are good hunting grounds for cheap and attractive bits of glass. Remember to make use of colours and themes by putting Frosted or Fondant Grapes into a green glass, Strawberry Cushions into a pink powder bowl or, for contrast, whirls of white meringue in a black glass cigarette box.

Unusual boxes are a real find – don't worry too

much about their condition or surface, provided they are not irretrievably rusty or covered with grime that won't wash off. You can paint them, or paper them with gift paper or the kind of patterned paper that is used for walls in dolls' houses – it comes in tiny brick and trellis designs which are perfect for small desserts.

Flat-bottomed boxes can be shallow or deep. Shallow ones will usually take one layer of tiny desserts; if you use a deep box that will take two layers, adjust the recipes and decorations so that the cakes or macaroons on the bottom have flattish tops that won't be harmed by the stiff paper between the layers.

Don't be put off if you don't like colours or patterns on the containers – spray paints are quick and cheerful and plenty of pretty stencil designs are available if you really want to go to town; making the most of containers can become as much fun as making the desserts.

Think, too, about all kinds of unusual containers. Use decorative coasters as miniature trays to present individual cakes. Fill sake cups from a Japanese souvenir shop with puddings, and stand them in a lacquer-painted cardboard box. A wire stationery tray is a marvellous container for a generous

present of cakes or biscuits; it is simple to spray it in enamel to complement the desserts, and, of course, it can be used later. Straw cheese platters are perfect for an assortment of cheesecakes. The sections of a cutlery tray can be filled with Sponge Fingers, Cinnamon Doughnuts and Coffee Kisses.

Garden shops are an endless source of suitable containers. Plastic drip trays can be sprayed and decorated, while ceramic ones are particularly fresh and bright in white and pastel colours. Plant pots come in so many sizes that there are usually one or two possibilities for each dessert.

Keep highly decorated novelties separate and protected in small, divided trays intended for growing seedlings. Support them on crumpled, coloured foil. For a particularly lavish present, make pretty paper 'packet' signs for a window-box drip tray of desserts and tape them on to the edge at intervals as if it was a miniature seed garden.

Fruit trays in thin wood are appropriate for Apple Strudels or Berry Tartlets. Varnish the wood for extra appeal and tie a bandanna around one corner. Simple baking trays are inexpensive, especially in bright, old-fashioned tin. Make the most of the glitter and decorate the trays with Mexican stencil designs leaving plenty of bare metal to shine through. The rims of the trays should keep the desserts from sliding off, and you can make a criss-cross handle in rope. Pierce holes through the base at each corner, and thread the rope through, knotting it at the top to keep it secure.

Other people's hobbies may be the inspiration for a container. A yachting enthusiast would appreciate a toy boat crammed with 'life savers' of tiny ring American Doughnuts. An ardent gardener should enjoy a lawn of artificial grass covered with a scattering of Spiced Flowers. A gourmet would appreciate some of the more difficult-to-make miniatures: tiny Lime Baskets, Chocolate-Coated Strawberries and a jar of Damson Compote with Armagnac.

You can also combine desserts with more practical presents: a jar of prepared fruit and a miniature bottle of complementary liqueur with a flambé dish, or tiny soufflés (and a jar of fruit sauce to serve with them) with a set of individual soufflé dishes. Both of these are only for people who will be able to use the ingredients quickly, but a tall glass jar filled with Prunes in Port, Pears with Gin and Lime Juice or Cherries in Red Wine will keep in the refrigerator for a few weeks.

Make an attractive label, to complement the packaging, and also include instructions for use, and a 'use by' date. Make edible Lebkuchen labels by cutting the dough into oblongs then placing them on a baking sheet and making a hole, with a skewer, ½ inch (1cm) from one end, in the centre of the biscuit. Press out the hole again after baking. When cold, pipe a decorative border in royal icing and, using a paper piping bag filled with a fine writing tube, write the recipient's name in icing. Thread ribbon through the hole and tie it on to the present.

Special Occasions

A new neighbour who has not had time to prepare any food would welcome an appropriate gift from your kitchen: a copy of the local newspaper wrapped around a foil container of Danish Pastries: Stars, Tivolis, Spandauers and Pinwheels.

Festive occasions are, of course, the best times for pulling out all the stops. Fill a ring mould with Christmas Puddings and decorate each with a tiny holly leaf and white icing frosting. Make traditional Lebkuchen Stars and Hearts and hang them on a miniature Christmas tree. Pack an assortment of Mince Pies on to a turkey platter and hold them in

place with cling film wrapped around with feather-patterned ribbons. Miniature Crèmes à la Coeur make an edible Valentine card for February 14, while, for Easter, tiny meringues pack nicely into a gold-foil Easter egg.

Finally, what about an assortment of finishing touches for a friend who is also an enthusiastic cook? Frosted Rose Petals or Mint Leaves, Chocolate Butterflies and Leaves, Meringue Stars and Glazed Lemon Peel Strands will all help to transform cakes and meringues, creams and jellies, fritters and crêpes into miniature desserts.

Creating Miniature Desserts

Sauces, creams, icings and other accompaniments and decorations can be inventively combined to create desserts that are as good to look at as they are to eat. This chapter includes basic recipes and also information about how to make – and apply – finishing touches to the desserts.

Basic Recipes

Apricot Glaze

Use to coat cakes and pastries before covering with Quick Fondant Icing, or to coat fruit in flans.

½ pound (200g) apricot jam
Juice of 1 lemon
2 tablespoons (2 × 15ml spoons) water

Place the jam, lemon juice and water in a saucepan. Stir over a low heat until the jam melts, then cook for 1 minute. Press through a nylon sieve and store in a covered jar. To use, warm the glaze and brush over the cake or fruit.

Butters

Brandy Butter

8 portions

2 ounces (50g) unsalted butter, softened
2 ounces (50g) caster sugar
4 tablespoons (4 × 15ml spoons) brandy

Beat butter and sugar together with an electric whisk, if possible, until they are pale and fluffy. Add the brandy a few drops at a time, whisking continuously until the mixture is light and fluffy.
   Pile into a small dish and serve chilled.

Rum Butter

Make as for Brandy Butter, replacing the caster sugar with moist dark brown sugar and the brandy with dark rum. Beat in ¼ teaspoon (½ × 2.5ml spoon) ground cinnamon.

Creams

Diplomat Cream

½ pint (250ml)

Traditionally used in patisserie as a filling, this cream can be flavoured and used in many of the same ways as whipped cream. It has more taste, but is less rich.

1 tablespoon (1 × 15ml spoon) custard powder
2 teaspoons (2 × 5ml spoons) Vanilla Sugar
   (page 151)
¼ pint (125ml) milk
¼ pint (125ml) double cream

Blend custard powder and sugar with milk in a saucepan. Bring to boil stirring and cook for 1 minute. Pour into a small basin and cover the surface with cling film to prevent a skin forming. Leave until cold then chill.
   Whisk the cream until thick. Gradually whisk in the custard and any flavouring.

Liqueur
Add 3 tablespoons (3 × 15ml spoons) of liqueur, brandy or rum.

Fruit
Add the finely grated rind of a small orange or lemon.

Coffee
Add 1 tablespoon (1 × 15ml spoon) instant coffee with the milk.

Chocolate
Add 2 ounces (50g) grated plain dessert chocolate to the hot cooked custard.

Left *Selection of decorations for miniature desserts.*

Pastry Cream (Crème Patissière)

Also called French Pastry Cream and Confectioner's Custard. Use this filling for pastries, cakes and flans.

½ pint (250ml)

½ pint (250ml) milk
1 vanilla pod
2 egg yolks
2 ounces (50g) caster sugar
1 ounce (25g) flour

Place the milk and vanilla pod in a small saucepan and bring slowly to boil. Whisk the egg yolks and sugar together until thick, then beat in the flour. Strain a little of the milk into the egg mixture then add the remainder, whisking all the time. Return the mixture to the saucepan and bring slowly to boil, whisking continuously. Cook about 1 minute then pour into a basin and cover the surface with cling film to prevent a skin forming. Cool then chill until required.

Rich Butter Cream

Use this cream to fill cakes and to decorate biscuits and pastries. Cover closely with cling film before storing in the refrigerator.

2 ounces (50g) granulated sugar
1 egg yolk
5 ounces (125g) unsalted butter

Place 6 tablespoons (6 × 15ml spoons) water in a small saucepan with the sugar. Stir over a low heat until the sugar has dissolved then boil for about 5 minutes until the syrup registers 220°F (104°C), the thread stage, on a sugar thermometer. To test, dip a teaspoon (5ml spoon) in the syrup, cool slightly, then press another spoon into the syrup on the back of the spoon. Pull the spoons apart. If a thread forms, the syrup is ready.

Whisk the egg yolk in a small basin and gradually whisk in the sugar syrup to make a soft mousse. Continue whisking until it is cold. Beat the butter until soft, then gradually whisk in the egg mousse a little at a time. Flavour as below.

Vanilla
Use Vanilla Sugar (page 151) or add a few drops of vanilla extract.

Lemon, Orange or Lime
Add 1 teaspoon (1 × 5ml spoon) finely grated rind and 1 tablespoon (1 × 15ml spoon) juice.

Chocolate
Add 1 ounce (25g) grated dessert chocolate to the egg yolk with the hot syrup.

Coffee
Add 1 teaspoon (1 × 5ml spoon) instant coffee dissolved in 2 teaspoons (2 × 5ml spoons) boiling water.

Praline
Add 1 ounce (25g) Praline (page 149).

Liqueur
Add 2 tablespoons (2 × 15ml spoons) strongly flavoured liqueur.

Green Marzipan

Use a skewer to stab green colouring into a piece of white marzipan, of the size required, then knead the marzipan until smooth and evenly coloured.

Icings

Chocolate Fudge Icing

Use to fill and frost cakes and pastries. Cover with cling film and store in the refrigerator until required.

4 ounces (100g) plain dessert chocolate
2 ounces (50g) butter
1 egg, beaten
6 ounces (150g) icing sugar, sifted

Break up the chocolate and place with the butter in a basin over a saucepan of hot, but not boiling, water. Stir occasionally until melted then gradually beat in the egg.

Remove the basin from the heat and beat in the sugar.

Note
Add less icing sugar if a smooth, flowing icing is required. Add up to 2 ounces (50g) more icing sugar to make a thick icing for swirling on cakes.

Storage
It is often impractical to make small quantities of these standard recipes. Make a 'normal' size batch each time, and store in the refrigerator or freezer.

Glacé Icing

Sufficient to coat the top of one 5in (12.5cm) cake

5 ounces (125g) icing sugar
1 tablespoon (1 × 15ml spoon) boiling water
1 teaspoon (1 × 5ml spoon) lemon juice
Food colouring, optional

Sift the icing sugar into a small basin, add the water and lemon juice and mix to form a thick icing which coats the back of the spoon.

Add food colouring, if desired: dip a skewer into the colouring and shake one drop into the icing. Mix and repeat until the desired colour is made.

To use, place the bowl of icing in a saucepan of boiling water and stir gently. Pour or spoon over the cake and spread with the back of the spoon. Leave until set.

Lemon
Replace the boiling water with lemon juice.

Orange
Replace the boiling water with orange juice and the lemon juice with orange flower water.

Coffee
Replace the boiling water and lemon juice with strong black coffee.

Quick Fondant Icing

Use to coat cakes, petits fours, tartlets and biscuits and fruits.

10 ounces (250g) icing sugar
2 to 3 tablespoons (2 to 3 × 15ml spoons) warmed
  Sugar Syrup (page 150)
Food colouring, optional

Sift the icing sugar into a bowl and beat in sufficient warm sugar syrup until the icing coats the back of the spoon or is the necessary consistency.

Tint with food colourings, if desired, and knead flavourings into the sugar paste.

Note
The icing can be left to set, then stored. To use, chop the set fondant and then put in a cup or bowl in a saucepan of boiling water, with Sugar Syrup. Stir occasionally until the fondant has melted. A ratio of 1 ounce (25g) fondant to 1 teaspoon (1 × 5ml spoon) syrup gives a good coating consistency.

Royal Icing

1 egg white
6 ounces (150g) icing sugar

Mix the egg white and icing sugar until they are the consistency of thick cream, then beat with a wooden spoon until the icing stands in stiff peaks.

Keep the bowl covered with a damp cloth, then use to cover cakes and for piping decorations.

Shiny Chocolate Icing

Sufficient to cover the top and sides of one 5in (12.5cm) cake

3 ounces (75g) plain dessert chocolate
2 tablespoons (2 × 15ml spoons) boiling water
1 teaspoon (1 × 5ml spoon) corn oil
1 tablespoon (1 × 15ml spoon) caster sugar

Break up the chocolate and place with the water, oil and sugar in a small basin over a saucepan of hot, but not boiling, water. Leave until the chocolate has melted then stir gently to mix.

Pour over the cake or dip biscuits and pastries in the icing.

Pink Marzipan

Make as for Green Marzipan (page 148), using pink food colouring.

Praline

Use to flavour Chantilly Cream, Rich Butter Cream and Meringues.

2 ounces (50g) unblanched almonds
2 ounces (50g) caster sugar

Prepare a baking sheet with a light brush of oil. Put the almonds and sugar in a small heavy saucepan and heat slowly until the sugar melts and turns pale golden brown. Gently stir to coat the nuts in caramel and continue cooking until it turns deep golden brown. Quickly turn out on to the oiled tin and leave until cold.

Crush to a fine powder using a pestle and mortar, a rolling pin, or put in a liquidizer.

Store in a tightly closed jar for up to three months.

Sugar Syrup

Use to add to chocolate for piping, to mix with liqueur and fruit juices, to soak and moisten cakes and for Quick Fondant Icing (page 149).

1/4 teaspoon (1/2 × 2.5ml spoon) cream of tartar
8 ounces (200g) granulated sugar

Dissolve the cream of tartar in 1 teaspoon (1 × 5ml spoon) water.

Dissolve the granulated sugar in 1/4 pint (125ml) of water in a small heavy saucepan over a low heat stirring occasionally. Increase the heat and bring to boil. Add the cream of tartar then boil until the syrup reaches the thread stage of 220°F (104°C) on a sugar thermometer. To test, dip a teaspoon in the syrup, cool slightly, then press another spoon into the syrup on the back of the spoon. Pull the spoons apart. If a thread forms, the syrup is ready.

Remove from the heat, cool and strain into a jar. The syrup can be stored for up to two months in a jar and does not need refrigerating.

Sauces

Custard Sauce

For speed, follow the directions on a packet of custard powder and make to the desired consistency with milk and sugar. For a finer flavour, try this recipe.

4 portions

1/2 pint (250ml) milk
1 vanilla pod
2 egg yolks
2 ounces (50g) caster sugar
1 teaspoon (1 × 5ml spoon) flour

Place the milk and vanilla pod in a small saucepan and bring slowly to boil.

Meanwhile, cream the yolks, sugar and flour together in a basin, gradually add the flavoured milk, then return to the saucepan and stir over a low heat until the sauce almost boils.

Remove from the heat, take out the vanilla pod and pour the sauce into a serving boat.

Rinse the vanilla pod, leave to dry in a warm place, then re-use.

Fruit Sauce

Follow this recipe when using peaches, apricots, nectarines, plums, damsons, also pineapple.

1/2 pint (250ml)

1/2 pound (200g) prepared fruit
4 tablespoons (4 × 15ml spoons) wine (red for red fruits, white for pale fruits)
2 ounces (50g) sugar
1 tablespoon (1 × 15ml spoon) Armagnac
2 to 3 tablespoons (2 to 3 × 15ml spoons) Sugar Syrup (left)

Cook the fruit gently in wine in a small saucepan. Liquidize and sieve if necessary. Return to the saucepan and add sugar, stir over a low heat until dissolved, then boil for 1/2 to 1 minute. Leave to cool then add the Armagnac and adjust the consistency with Sugar Syrup. If desired, use an extra 1 ounce (25g) chopped fruit, remove with a draining spoon before liquidizing, then return to the sauce after cooling.

Jam Sauce

Use apricot, strawberry, raspberry or plum jam, or orange or lime marmalade.

1/2 pint (250ml)

4 ounces (100g) jam
3 tablespoons (3 × 15ml spoons) lemon or lime juice
6 to 8 tablespoons (6 to 8 × 15ml spoons) Sugar Syrup (above left)
2 tablespoons (2 × 15ml spoons) spirit or liqueur

Heat the jam gently in a small pan with the lemon juice and Sugar Syrup and stir until melted. Sieve, if necessary, then stir in the spirit or liqueur. Adjust the consistency with more sugar syrup, if necessary.

Use brandy or Armagnac for apricot sauce, Cointreau for strawberry sauce, kirsch or kümmel for raspberry sauce, slivowitch with plum jam, whisky or Drambuie with orange marmalade and white wine with lime marmalade. Add 1 ounce (25g) chopped ginger to marmalade sauce, if desired.

Soft-Fruit Sauce

This recipe is suitable for raspberries, loganberries, blackberries, tayberries, mulberries, cranberries and strawberries.

½ pint (250ml)

½ pound (250g) fruit
2 ounces (50g) sugar
2 to 3 tablespoons (2 to 3 × 15ml spoons) Sugar Syrup (far left)
1 tablespoon (1 × 15ml spoon) liqueur (optional)

Place fruit in a small saucepan and heat until the juice runs. Add the sugar and stir to dissolve. Bring to boil and cook quickly for about ½ minute. Sieve and cool. Add Sugar Syrup and liqueur to reach the required consistency.

Use kirsch for raspberries and loganberries, Grand Marnier for strawberries, mulberries and loganberries, port for cranberries and crème de cassis for blackberries. Add 1 ounce (25g) whole fruit just before serving, if desired.

To freeze fruit sauces
Pour the sauce into ice-cube trays or small 2 fl oz (50ml) containers. Pack in plastic bags, seal and freeze. To thaw, heat gently for serving hot; thaw at room temperature for serving cold.

Hot Chocolate Sauce

About ¼ pint (125ml)

4 ounces (100g) plain chocolate, chopped
1 ounce (25g) icing sugar
½ ounce (15g) unsalted butter, chopped

Place all the ingredients in a bowl with 2 fluid ounces (50 ml) hot water and place over a pan of hot water.

Heat until the chocolate has melted, stir well and serve hot or warm.

Vanilla Sugar

Make this for flavouring ice creams, cakes, Chantilly Cream and sweet pastry.

2 vanilla pods
½ pound (200g) caster sugar

Cut up the vanilla pods into four or five pieces and bury in the sugar in a jar. Cover securely and store in the cupboard for two days to allow the flavour to penetrate the sugar.

The sugar will keep for up to a year before the flavour fades.

Finishing Touches

Chocolate Decorations

Various types of chocolate are available and it is important to choose the right one.

Plain dessert chocolate, also called couverture, has the best flavour and should be used when flavouring desserts or in decorations where there is a considerable amount of chocolate. The disadvantage of this type of chocolate is that it will not set after melting unless it is first 'tempered'. This involves heating, cooling and stirring the chocolate to make the two different crystals in cocoa butter compatible before the chocolate is cooled to the working temperature of 88°F (31°C) for dark chocolate and 87°F (30.5°C) for milk chocolate and white chocolate.

To temper chocolate

Use a minimum of 10 ounces (250g). Chop two-thirds and grate the remainder. Place the chopped chocolate in a small saucepan or bowl that will completely fit over another saucepan, leaving no space for steam to spoil the chocolate. Pour some hot but not boiling water into the lower saucepan and melt the chopped chocolate above it away from the heat, stirring occasionally. The top saucepan or bowl must not touch the water and must just feel warm. Place a thermometer in the chocolate and remove the bowl from the heat when the temperature registers 100°F (38°C). The lumps may not all be melted. Dry the bottom of the pan or bowl then add the grated chocolate. Give it a good stir then heat it up to 88°F (31°C), stirring all the time until it becomes smooth. Try not to beat in any air. Leave for 5 minutes off the heat, stir, then re-heat and keep the chocolate at 88°F (31°C). To see if it has tempered, dip a dry, cold knife in the chocolate. It should set hard on the knife and crack when broken off.

Chocolate-Flavoured Cake Covering

This is available in dark, milk and white. It contains vegetable fat which makes it easy to handle and it can be used without tempering. Its disadvantage is its poor flavour and waxy texture. Use it only for tiny decorations such as Chocolate Leaves (opposite).

If time is short, you can mix dessert chocolate with chocolate-flavoured cake covering, but take care to keep the temperature low.

Chocolate Cases

Use small paper cake cases, dariole moulds, brioche or patty tins, cream horn tins, etc.

If using non-metal containers, cover them in a layer of cling film to ensure easy removal of the chocolate case.

For 6 Chocolate Cases use 3 ounces (75g) chocolate. With a small brush paint the *inside* of the paper cases, brioche or patty tins and dariole moulds with a layer of tempered dark, milk or white chocolate. Paint the *outside* of cream horn tins and shell shapes with chocolate. Invert on to greaseproof paper and leave the chocolate to set. Repeat until three layers of chocolate have been completed. Leave to set hard in refrigerator, then carefully slip the chocolate case from the tin.

Chocolate Shells

Use tiny scallop shells covered with a layer of cling film. Prise the chocolate from the shell when set, and ease away the cling film.

For larger quantities

Use extra chocolate and fill the metal cases to the brim with melted chocolate, pour away excess and leave to set upside down on a wire tray.

Chocolate Curls

Spread tempered dark, milk or white chocolate on a cold work surface and leave until almost hard. Using a sharp, straight-bladed knife, draw the knife at an angle of 45° across the chocolate, shaving off a curl. Leave the curls to harden in the refrigerator. Alternatively, use a potato peeler or knife to shave off the flat side of a bar of cake covering.

Chocolate Flakes

Prepare dark, milk or white chocolate as for Chocolate Curls, then simply scrape off flakes of chocolate, over a piece of non-stick baking parchment, or grate the chocolate directly over the dessert or gâteau.

Chocolate Hearts

Spread tempered dark, milk or white chocolate thinly over a piece of smooth non-stick baking parchment or waxed paper. Leave until chocolate is dry but not hard. Using small, heart-shaped petits fours cutters, cut out shapes. Slide paper on to a baking sheet and place in the refrigerator to harden the chocolate. Peel away the parchment or paper and store in a small container in the refrigerator.

Chocolate Leaves

Wash and dry small leaves. Using a fine paint brush, lightly coat the underside of the leaves with tempered dark, milk or white chocolate-flavoured cake covering. Leave to dry, chocolate side uppermost, on waxed paper or non-stick baking parchment. Place in the refrigerator to set. Carefully peel off the leaves and store in small containers in the refrigerator.

Chocolate Rolls

Spread tempered chocolate thinly over a marble slab or clean modern work surface. When dry, but not hard, make rolls by pushing (or pulling) a long-bladed straight-edged knife held at a slight angle across the top of the chocolate to make thin rolls. Store in a small box in the refrigerator.

Chocolate Shapes

Spread tempered dark, milk or white chocolate thinly over waxed paper or smooth non-stick baking parchment. Leave until the chocolate is dry but not hard, then cut out shapes using small petits fours cutters. Slide paper on to a baking sheet and leave in the refrigerator while it hardens. Peel away the paper or parchment and store the shapes in a small box in the refrigerator.

Geometric shapes: squares, triangles, wedges

Use about 3 ounces (75g) tempered chocolate for sixteen 1½in (4cm) squares or 32 triangles or 24 wedges.

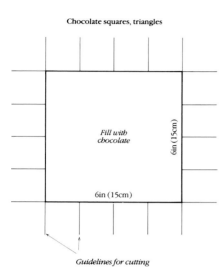

Chocolate squares, triangles

Fill with chocolate

6in (15cm)

6in (15cm)

Guidelines for cutting

On a smooth piece of non-stick baking parchment draw a 6in (15cm) square. Mark along each side at 1½in (4cm) intervals and draw lines outwards at right-angles. Alternatively, draw three 5in (12.5cm) circles and divide each into 8 equal wedges. Extend the lines well beyond the circle or square. Turn the parchment over and place on a flat surface. Secure this firmly to the surface using sticky tape or drawing pins.

Spread melted chocolate evenly over the parchment within the marked lines. Leave the chocolate to dry.

With a straight-bladed knife cut the chocolate into squares or wedge-shaped portions using the extended lines as a guide. Cut the squares diagonally to make triangles. Chill and store in the refrigerator, in a small container.

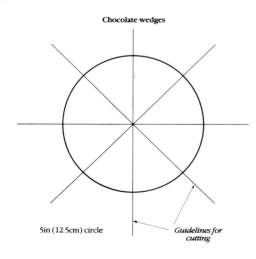

Chocolate wedges

5in (12.5cm) circle

Guidelines for cutting

Oblongs

To make an oblong, use about 2 ounces (50g) chocolate and draw a 6 × 3in (15 × 7.5cm) oblong on the baking parchment, then continue as above.

Note

The size of the basic shape on the paper, and of squares, triangles, etc can be altered to suit different recipes. For example, for twenty-five 1in (2.5cm) squares, draw a 5in (12.5cm) square.

To Pipe Chocolate

Use Piping Chocolate to decorate cakes, etc or for various motifs. White chocolate can be coloured for extra effect. Colour as for Quick Fondant Icing (page 149) but use powdered colourings.

Draw shapes on a smooth piece of non-stick baking parchment. Reverse the parchment and secure with sticky tape or drawing pins.

Paper Piping Bag

Suitable paper
Non-stick baking parchment
Good-quality greaseproof paper
Waxed paper

Cut a piece of paper 10 × 8in (25 × 20cm) (A). Fold and cut in half diagonally to make two triangles each with a blunt corner (B).

Hold the middle of the long side of one of the triangles with the left hand and with your right hand fold the blunt corner Y round in front to just below point X, to form a cone (C).

Holding the pointed end of the cone in the left hand, twist corner Z round the cone and up behind cone to corner X (D).

Fold the extra paper at the top down twice to secure the cone (E).

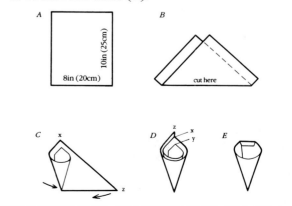

A

10in (25cm)

8in (20cm)

B

cut here

C

x

D

z x y

E

z

Piping Chocolate

4 ounces (100g) chocolate
1 ounce (25g) icing sugar
A few drops of water

Melt the chocolate and stir in the icing sugar. Add a few drops of water to give a thick piping consistency, which should fall heavily from the spoon. Alternatively, for large quantities, beat in Sugar Syrup (page 150) until the required consistency is reached.

Place the chocolate in a small paper icing bag (page 153). Fold over the top and snip off the end to the thickness of the piping required and gently squeeze out the chocolate round the shapes, holding the bag about 1in (2.5cm) above the paper.

Leave until the chocolate is dry but not hard, then store in a small box in the refrigerator.

Always pipe extra shapes or motifs to allow for breakages.

Chocolate Butterflies

With Raised Wings

After drawing the shape on non-stick baking parchment, using dark Piping Chocolate, pipe a line round the edge of each wing. Still using a piping bag, fill the centre of each wing with chocolate. Leave to dry, then peel off the paper.

Pipe a thick line of white chocolate about ½in (1.25cm) long on to baking parchment or waxed paper. Arrange wings standing up on each side. Support them with small rolls made from kitchen paper and leave until the chocolate has set. Pipe antennae when completely dry; carefully peel off the paper. Store in a small box in the refrigerator.

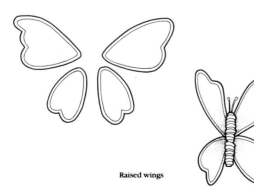

Raised wings

Flat Butterfly

Pipe wings as described. When dry, pipe a thick line of chocolate down the centre with added antennae.

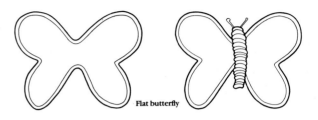

Flat butterfly

Pink Chocolate Butterfly

Proceed as for the variations above, but fill the centre of each wing with white chocolate to which powdered pink colouring has been added. See Quick Fondant Icing (page 149) for method.

Chocolate Motifs

Pipe a line from A to B, then in a clockwise direction pipe oval shapes increasing in size but keeping the bases at the same point.

Coloured Crystals

Sprinkle these crystals over meringues before baking, or over glacé iced cakes and biscuits and whipped cream immediately before serving.

2 rounded tablespoons (4 × 15ml spoons)
*   granulated sugar*
A few drops of food colouring

Place the sugar and 2 or 3 drops of food colouring in a small bowl. Using a small palette knife, work the crystals against each other until the sugar is evenly coloured. Spread the sugar over a piece of greaseproof paper or non-stick baking parchment and leave to dry in a warm place.

Store in a dry, screw-topped jar.

Frosted Leaves, Flowers

Suitable flowers are flat, thin-petalled flowers such as roses (not Christmas roses), primroses, pansies, sweet peas, nasturtiums, forget-me-nots, lilac and violets, also fruit blossoms such as apple, pear and cherry. Individual petals, such as rose petals, can also be frosted.

Suitable leaves are rose, mint, sage, thyme, lemon balm, French parsley, lamb's tongue.

Note

Some flowers, including bulb flowers, are inedible so if in doubt, remove before eating the dessert.

1 egg white
2 teaspoons (2 × 5ml spoons) water
Caster sugar, to coat

Prepare the items to be frosted. Pick flowers and leaves just before using.

Flowers

Shake lightly upside down then spread out on kitchen paper and leave 15 minutes (to encourage any insects to crawl out).

Leaves

Gently wash and dry leaves on kitchen paper. Spread out to dry thoroughly. Avoid bruising leaves.

Place egg white and water in a small basin and beat together until the egg white is no longer stringy but not too frothy. Using a fine paint-brush, paint the under and top side of the petals or leaves with a thin layer of egg white, making sure they are evenly yet not thickly coated. Sprinkle lightly with caster sugar.

Spread the frosted items on greaseproof paper or non-stick baking parchment and leave to dry in an airy place but away from direct sunlight which would bleach the colour. Store between sheets of tissue paper for up to four weeks for leaves, two weeks for flowers.

Note

Some flowers will darken or go limp if their petals are bruised or if the flowers are not at their peak when picked. Discard these. It is sensible to frost more flowers than are needed because they are very fragile.

Glazed Citrus Peel Strands

Suitable fruits are oranges, lemons, limes, grapefruit. Choose firm fruit with a good colour and a rough skin.

1 orange or 1 lemon or 2 limes
3 fluid ounces (75ml) water
2 ounces (50g) granulated sugar

Scrub fruit with a small brush under running water. Using a potato peeler or small vegetable knife shave off long strips of peel down the length of the fruit, avoiding the white pith. Place the peel on a chopping board and cut into thin strips with a sharp knife.

Place the water in a small saucepan and bring to boil. Add the peel, reduce heat, cover and simmer for 1 or 2 minutes until the peel is tender. Remove with a draining spoon. Add the sugar to the pan and stir until dissolved. Increase the heat and cook rapidly until the syrup is reduced by half. Return the peel to the pan and continue cooking uncovered, stirring occasionally, until well glazed. Remove the peel and gently shake off any excess syrup. Leave the peel on non-stick baking parchment or greaseproof paper to cool. When cold, store in a small jar or box between pieces of waxed paper.

To glaze fruit slices

Small slices of oranges, lemons, limes and kumquats can be glazed as above.

Marzipan Cut-Outs

Flowers

Six 1½in (4cm) flowers

6–8 ounces (150–200g) Green Marzipan (page 148)
Icing sugar

Roll out Green Marzipan and trim to 4 × 14in (10 × 35cm). Cut down its length into three 1¼in (3cm) strips, then cut twelve 1¼in (3cm) leaf shapes diagonally from each strip. Sprinkle six individual tartlet tins with icing sugar and press six leaves, slightly overlapping, into each. Leave several hours, until the marzipan has set, then remove from the tins and leave to dry overnight.

Leaves

About 24 leaves

2 ounces (50g) Green Marzipan (page 148)
Icing sugar
Melted chocolate

Lightly dust work surface with sifted icing sugar. Knead marzipan until smooth, then roll out to ⅛in (6mm) thick. Use a shaped leaf cutter to cut out as many shapes as possible. Lift leaves from the work surface with a small palette knife and place them on greaseproof paper or non-stick baking parchment. Mark veins with a knife before leaving to dry. To curve leaves, place them over the handles of wooden spoons.

To decorate, brush melted chocolate over half or the complete top surface of each leaf, or pipe a thin line of chocolate down the centre to represent a vein. Store between layers of greaseproof paper or baking parchment in a cardboard box.

Note
If no cutters are available, roll out the marzipan and cut into ¾in (2cm) strips. Cut each strip diagonally at ¾in (2cm) intervals. Shape the edges of each to form a leaf. Lightly mark the veins of the leaf with a pointed knife; leave to dry, then decorate as above.

Hearts, Daisies

2 ounces (50g) Pink Marzipan (page 149)
Icing sugar

Roll out marzipan as for leaves and cut out shapes using a petits fours cutter. Alternatively, use a small fluted cutter for daisies and a small round plain cutter for hearts and shape edges where necessary. Store as for leaves.

Piped Cream Decorations

Piped cream can be used either as a single star or an elaborate design. Whipped cream freezes well and can also be used on frozen desserts.

Whip any spare cream with a little sugar – about 1 teaspoon (1 × 5ml spoon) to 6 tablespoons (6 × 15ml spoons) double cream – and pipe stars or whirls on a baking sheet. Once frozen, these motifs can be stored in a box interleaved with non-stick baking parchment or waxed paper and used as instant decoration.

To whip cream
For best results use a mixture of double and single creams, 2 parts double to 1 part single, or use whipping cream.

Chill the cream, bowl and balloon or hand whisk before using. An electric whisk can over-whip the cream and can cause it to separate. Whip quickly at first until the cream has a matt-looking surface, then whip slowly until it stands in soft peaks and does not fall off the upturned whisk. When whipped, the cream should have doubled in volume.

To pipe the cream
Piping tends to 'frill' the cream, especially if it has been over-whipped, and warmth from your hand can quickly turn it to butter. Whip cream in small batches, and use a clean, cold bag and piping tube. Large nylon piping bags are available with a large plain or star Savoy or potato tube.

Fold the piping bag back on itself about half way down and stand in a cup or beaker for easy filling. Place only a few tablespoons (15ml spoons) of whipped cream in the bag at one time. Pull the top of the piping bag up and fold over to enclose the cream. Press from the top of the bag and avoid cradling the bag in the palm of the hand, which will over-heat the cream. If the cream 'frills' or separates, wash and dry the bag and start again.

Toasted Nuts

Suitable nuts
Blanched almonds – whole, flaked, chopped
Hazelnuts – whole, chopped
Mixed chopped nuts

Prepare a medium-hot grill. Remove the rack and line the grill pan with foil. Spread the nuts over the foil and toast until evenly browned, occasionally stirring the nuts and turning them over to ensure even toasting. This will take only a few seconds depending on the quantity of nuts being toasted. Lift the foil out of the pan and leave the nuts to cool. Rub off the hazelnut skins between two pieces of kitchen paper, if necessary.

The cold nuts can be stored for a few days in a screw-topped jar, but are best used the same day.

Index

Page numbers in *italic* refer to the illustrations

Picture acknowledgments

Edmund Goldspink page 111
David Burch page 2
All other photographs by
David Jordan

Colour separations by
Anglia Reproductions